STANDING ON SINKING SAND

Make the Rest of Your Time the Best and Reach Your Life Goals

---

Stephanie J. Womack

STANDING ON SINKING SAND

Copyright © 2016 by Virtue Communications, LLC

All rights reserved. No part of this book may be reproduced or transmitted in any form or by any means without written permission from the author.

ISBN 978-0-692-81909-8

Printed in USA by 48HrBooks (www.48HrBooks.com)

Dedication

To the past, thank you for teaching me. To the present, thank you for keeping me. To the future, thank you for waiting on me.

Table of Contents

Introduction 5

Overcome FEAR on Purpose 9

PIVOT with Intention 31

Create SPACE for God 53

SPARK Your Higher Self 71

BUILD Your Brand 92

Action Plan Guide 114

Bonus: Time Audit Worksheet............................. 115

Bonus: WTF Journal Pages 116

Bonus: 7-Day SMART Goal Worksheet 128

Bonus: 30-Day SMART Goal Worksheet 129

Bonus: 50 Things to Throw Away Checklist 130

About the Author 132

Introduction

I have learned that I absolutely needed to let go of perfection. God doesn't need me to be perfect, he just needs me to be willing. He needs me to be myself so that this message can resonate with the someone that needs it, which means that there ~~may be~~ is some cussing (mild), there may be some jokes (I think they're funny, so that counts), and there may be some tears. But most of all, he needs me to let you know that you can do this, whatever this is and you don't have to do it alone.

These lessons come from my experiences in deciding to participate in God's plan for my life and discovering that I really had to do a lot of interior work, before I could get to the exterior that I present to you through my writing, speaking, and creative work. I have also learned that it's a process that has to be repeated over and over again. Not because you don't get it, but because you start to understand that you evolve as life takes you through things, but God's promises remain.

My goal is to lay out some simple lessons I've learned thus far about how to: overcome **FEAR** on purpose, **PIVOT** with intention, create **SPACE** for God to work, **SPARK** your higher self, and **BUILD** a brand that you love. I see this book as a faith-based branding guide. If you have followed my work, you know that I care a lot about personal branding. I present the visual below as a simple visual of what a personal brand is:

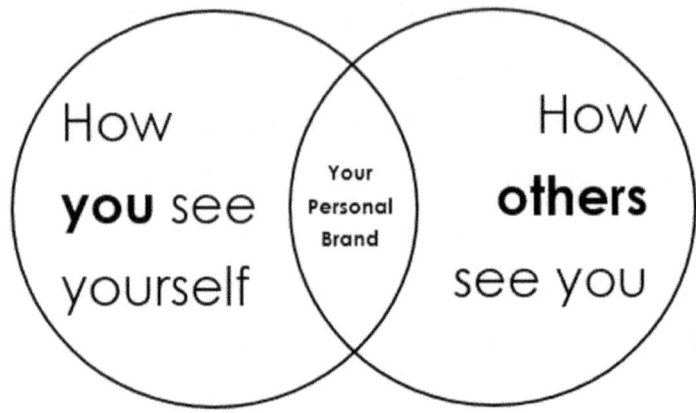

As you can see, there are two overlapping circles that make up your personal brand. Regardless of how others see you, you are the main component, while people's perception of it my change, you will always be there. But it takes work to build a brand that you can turn into your lifestyle and live out your personal goals and dreams. This work is about helping you manage your own PR (personal responsibility). And become your own brand ambassador. That work starts with an understanding and love of self.

All of these tools and tips are presenting as acronyms with thoughts, stories, or ideas presenting under each heading. The format is as follows: a promise from God with a short thought, story or idea followed by some homework. Some of these ideas may be new to you, some you may have heard before. I'm all about taking simple solutions to solve mundane challenges. In my experience, sometimes it takes someone to point out the simplicity of seemingly complex problems that we can't get a handle on. That's because our perspective of the situation is jaded. Sometimes life feels like you are standing on sinking sand, running out of time to do all the things you planned to do in your teens, 20s, 30s and beyond.

There's going to be a lot of homework and action steps to complete as you read and work through the book. If you do the work, you will walk away with a plan. This book means so much to me because I believe that it offers so much! I have designed it to hopefully meet you where you are. It is a Bible study guide, an action planner, and a journal prompter, but mostly, it's a rope for you to grab to keep you from sinking any further. It's a letter from me to you with a core message of love, self-love to be exact.

It's personal for me because there was once a time I didn't love myself. I struggled with self-esteem and not being happy because I placed that responsibility on others. I wasn't happy because I did all the things I was supposed to do and still wasn't fulfilled. I had to learn that it is my responsibility to decide to be happy and decide what my success looks like and decide how to make success my reality. I learned that I was letting my fear control me to the point where I didn't trust myself. There was a disconnect between what I was telling myself that I believed spiritually and what I actually felt.

My mission is to help you not only trust yourself, but love yourself enough to turn your life into a brand that you love to live. To trust yourself and love yourself, you have to be able to see yourself. I want this book to be your mirror. Some of this will require some tough love on my part. I have to tell you this now so you can manage your expectations. I also want you to know that, although I'm offering you some biblical principles, I'm convicted to give you a real world kick in the ass! This is not a judgment, it's an observation and lived through experiences.

If you are ready to stand on solid ground, trust what you know and do the work to become the powerhouse you are meant to be, we can absolutely do that together. I know you can do this and even more important, I know that deep inside, you want this too. I believe in you. I believe that somebody needs what you are keeping inside because you fear that no one has that same pain, but trust me, you are the testimony that someone needs. You are the new branch in your family tree that will break chains of poverty and mediocrity. I'm so ready for this and I know you are too. All you have to do it grab the rope!

Overcome FEAR on Purpose

- **F**ree your mind of negativity
- **E**liminate your excuses
- **A**ffirm your goals
- **R**eimagine your life

We don't have much time, so I'm going to start with the hard truth: fear is debilitating, and half the time we don't even realize we are under its siege. Fear causes us to create these habits that keep us, well habitually stuck. But, habits can be broken, and fear overcome. It just takes intentional effort.

If you believe in God, you should believe in his instructions and promises in the Bible. Even if you don't believe in God, you believe that there is a Higher Being at work in your life or that there are signs that lead and guide you to make decisions and give you confirmation. That energy you feel doesn't have a denomination, but the context of these lessons are biblical. The Bible is full of God's promises to us, but as humans, we get in the way of our own divinity, by not trusting the Spirit, and therefore not trusting ourselves.

One of God's promises that I stand on today is 2 Timothy 1:7: "For the Spirit God gave us does not make us timid, but gives us power, love and self-discipline." But, there was a time when I wasn't always so sure and felt that I didn't deserve to stand on this particular promise. Timid? But Lord, that's me! I'm an introvert! Power? Love? Yea, right.

For years, I played small with my faith (and opportunities) because of fear. You may be feeling some of these fears; fear of not being good enough. Fear of what others will think. Fear of failure. As if *that* isn't enough to bear, the deeply rooted seeds of fear will even have you think that you aren't worthy of the good things that happen to you, even when you know you work your ass off, we will talk about why later. But, if you're not careful, you'll develop a fear of being seen; a fear of being heard; a fear of being valuable. You will fear that people will see you've changed and make you feel a way, as if change is a bad thing.

This lesson is not new and helps set the foundation of this process to shift your mindset and prepare for what's to come. Now, I have the opportunity to provide more context behind this narrative, which has helped me get over myself when I'm stalling on something I know I should be doing or have already done related to life goals. If you catch nothing else, catch this one because it's universal to overcoming challenges.

These ideas are the catalyst for your story, which has already been written, but you're like Alice in Wonderland and think it can only exist in a dream. It's time to wake up and say hello to your magic. So many beliefs we hold true about ourselves are because someone else planted them there.

Remember, God didn't give you fear, man did. You no longer have time or permission to hold on to doubt, fear, low self-esteem, your mama's mistakes, your daddy's mistakes, your own mistakes or other people's deconstructive criticism. What you do have is, permission to say that enough is enough and embrace the ability you have to create change.

God's Promise: "For the Spirit God gave us does not make us timid, but gives us power, love and self-discipline." – 2 Timothy 1:7

Free Your Mind of Negativity

Do you constantly hear voices in your head? Of course. We all do. Communication scholars suggest that every communication experience involves six "voices." And these "voices" influence our perception of ourselves, which also informs the communication process we have with others. Your perception of yourself shapes how you communicate with yourself. If you have a negative perception, your inner voice is more critical, even over little things. If you live in this space, compliments from other people probably confuse you. Your personal brand is dependent on your self-perception. To understand your self-perception, you need to understand the following ideas and how they work together: self-concept, self-esteem and self-fulfilling prophecy.

Your self-concept is a constructed idea based on your beliefs about you and the responses of other people. Self-esteem is based on the value and confidence you have in the idea of yourself. A self-fulfilling prophecy is a predication that comes true because belief and behavior are congruent. Let's talk about beliefs for a moment. There are some beliefs that we have because they were taught to us, and others we have because we learned them over time from our own experiences and understanding.

Sometimes, as we grow older we challenge the beliefs that have been taught to us. Then, there are some beliefs we hold on to, even though they serve us no purpose. Like, limiting beliefs...but where do they come from? A belief is formed when information infiltrates our mental space and influences the way we interpret aspects of reality. As you have interacted with others and continue to do so, you internalize messages and learn how to communicate with them and yourself.

But it's the dialogue with yourself that I really want to talk about... This becomes self-talk. Research indicates that self-talk has a major impact on your self-concept and therefore your overall mental health. Self-talk helps to frame your self-perception. Let me run it by you like this, self-talk is what gives your fear power. You can either feel good about new things or really scared of it, based on how you talk yourself through it. Self-talk is not always bad, in fact it can be a good thing when it can be controlled and used as a coach to get you through challenges.

Considering all of this, self-talk ultimately has a huge impact on your personal brand because at least half of the equation is how you see yourself, which is largely controlled by how you talk to yourself. Confront your negative self-talk by making yourself aware of what you actually say to yourself. I had to learn that there's no praise like self-praise.

I remember a time that I had convinced myself that God had forgotten about me. That he forgot to give me a unique gift or talent that I could use to have an impact. One of my favorite sayings from the Bible now is that God will never leave nor forsake you. In complete transparency, I used to cry out and say WHY God, have you left me and forsaken me. I constantly and selfishly asked God "Why?"

In working on myself, I realized that asking God "Why" was a learned behavior because I had always been asked "Why." I remember very vivid times when I was younger, expressing a desire I had and being questioned about why I had that desire. I internalized those things and realized that I had talked myself out of a lot of things or played small because I didn't have all the answers to "Why?"

Of course, now I know that I don't need all the answers to get started. Internalizing made me feel like I wasn't good enough to tackle these things, especially as a young child, when everything seems so big and impossible. At that time, I didn't know the answer to the age-old question, "How do you eat an elephant?" (If you don't know the answer, read to the end). But I wanted to share that with you to help you realize that your negative self-talk is probably a reflection of someone else's inability to see their own magic. This is not an invitation to blame them, but rather an invitation to forgive.

By the way, you eat an elephant one piece at a time and that's what we're going to do together. The homework assignment for this step is to complete the **Positive Self-Talk**

Worksheet. If you've done this before, I want to give you a journal exercise to start doing. At the end of your day, write down all the things that frustrated you during the day, how did you feel? What did you say to yourself in those moments? Now, for every one thing that frustrated you, write two things that went well. Also, capture how you felt in those moments and what you said to yourself. Make this a daily habit, for the feel goods to outweigh the heaviness of those "ice cream for dinner" type days. Get ready to walk in your power.

Affirmation:

I AM LIVING PROOF OF GOD'S LOVE.

Quick Self-Talk Assessment

Negative things I say to myself on a daily basis:
_____
_____
_____
_____

Where do I think these negative beliefs come from:
_____
_____
_____
_____

Who do I need to forgive: (You can include yourself)
_____
_____
_____
_____

What steps do I need to take to forgive:
_____
_____
_____
_____

Positive Self-talk Worksheet (Goal Specific)

What would be the worst thing that could happen if I didn't do as well as I would like at:

Writing my blog: _____

Starting my nonprofit: _____

Launching my website: _____

Identify some additional ideas you have and give the worst and best things that could happen:

Goal/Idea	Worst that could happen	Best that could happen

Give 2 examples of negative self-talk that would keep you from accomplishing your goals:

_____

_____

_____

Now, give 4 examples of positive self-talk to replace those negative thoughts, *and* write down how you feel in that moment:

_____

_____

_____

_____

God's Promise: "Sluggards do not plow in season; so at harvest time they look but find nothing." – Proverbs 20:4

Eliminate Your Excuses

Fear makes it easy to create excuses that sound legit to an untrained ear. Don't be afraid to do God's will. If you are sure God told you to do something, don't be afraid to do it because He is always by your side. God promised that he would never leave nor forsake you, so why are you convinced that he will?

Did you know that Noah preached for 120 years...and not one person that he preached to believed him? Some of us can't wait 120 minutes for something to come to past. We know what happened to the people that ignored Noah, but can you imagine how he felt for all those years? I'm sure he was getting the side eye from the people and probably his family too at some point. I'm sure it would have been easier to say not today, Lord. But Noah stayed steadfast, built the ark and saved his family! Does your family tree need to be saved?

There's no record of Noah saying "I'll do it next week" or "I really don't have time." See, Noah was convicted to complete his task because it meant his salvation. Conviction means having a firmly held belief or opinion. He didn't know where or when, but he knew something big was going to happen and he believed.

What if your salvation depended on you accomplishing your life goals? Would that light a fire under you? I'm willing to bet that if we had the mental capacity to physically see salvation, that would make a difference. But, since we don't, let's talk about something you can see: your family tree. There's someone looking to you to change the trajectory of how the branches grow and how the leaves sway. You may not even know them yet or maybe won't even get to meet them, but they can't grow, if you don't plant.

A hundred and twenty years is more than enough time to get lazy and make excuses, but fortunately, you don't have that much time to waste. My sorority taught me that excuses are tools that build monuments of nothing. But I know you have a desire to be monumental. Do any of these sound familiar:

- I don't have the money I need to really make it happen the way I want to.
- I really don't have the extra time to make that happen.
- There's so many people already doing that. I'm not trying to be a copycat.
- I don't know how to get started, let me do more research.

Your brain is powerful and you can convince yourself of almost anything. Excuses will allow you to believe what you say even if it's not true. If you really think about it, excuses really aren't reasons. They are false justifications for why you won't do something. An unwillingness to be obedient and laziness will cause you to lose your harvest.

Bonus Promise*: "God cannot be mocked. A man reaps what he sows." – Galatians 6:7

Thinking back on when I first started working on my business, I avoided doing the things I knew I needed to do…and made a lot of excuses. I had to realize that I was unwilling to listen, so I filled my head with excuses as to not hear God's instructions. This meant I lacked clarity big time, which also meant I spent a lot of time in angst. And mad at God like, "Lord, why won't you speak you me?" ☺

I also spent a lot of time sharing my excuses with other people, so they too would be convinced and not call me out on my BS. As I started to put together my digital workbook, I was convicted while writing this section, so then I started keeping my excuses to myself. One of my go-to excuses was: no time. I was convinced that I had no time to do this thing that I felt God told me to do until I was asked to speak at a retreat…and had no content!

That speaking engagement gave me a deadline. That deadline meant I had the makings of a SMART goal, which meant I either needed to make time or decline the speaking gig. How would that have gone over? You want to be a speaker and writer yet won't take the time to write a speech. OK, Girl!

The point is this: no one has ever achieved a goal with lackluster effort, and neither will you! If you're waiting for more money or time, you won't be prepared when the season does come. To really eliminate your excuses, you need a plan. Take a few minutes to think about the fear (excuse) that you want to tackle rather quickly. Here's the homework: use the **Eliminate Your Excuses** worksheet to work through your fear. Think about specific actions that you can take within 1 week and 1 month to conquer this fear. You can use this information to create a SMART goal. A SMART goal is Specific, Measurable, Attainable, Realistic, and Time-Bound. I will share more about SMART goals as we go on.

Even if you have done this before using the workbook, this is a useful exercise anytime you are thinking of taking on a new challenge and feel unsure. I still use this to think through all my thoughts when I'm stalling on something. If you use the timeframes provided in the worksheet, you can then work backwards to create a plan to accomplish the 7-day and 30-day steps. And then, you repeat the process until the days turn into months and the months into a year from now and look what you've accomplished! Until you start walking in your power, you can't afford to be lazy.

Eliminate Your Excuses Worksheet

MY FEAR: _____

Be as specific as possible

Identify what is real about this fear, if anything.

_____
_____

Identify what is not real about this fear.

_____
_____

What can I change?

_____
_____

In *1 week*:

_____
_____

In *1 month*:

_____
_____

God's Promise: "Therefore everyone who hears these words of mine and puts them into practice is like a wise man who built his house on the rock." – Matthew 7: 24

Affirm Yourself

In my workbook, *4 Steps to Shift Your Mindset and Start Building Your Personal Brand*, I talk about the power of affirmations and how they have a profound effect on your self-talk. We talked about how saying is believing and how believing turns into your reality. That's the purpose of these affirmations. An affirmation is a declaration of the truth of something. Do you believe that the Bible is a true document? If so, you have to declare the truth and your purpose with boldness. This step is about making God's promises personal, so you'll be able to see yourself in these words as you move forward in the book.

It's about knowing that God loves you enough to provide instruction and encouragement in every area of your life. It's about loving yourself enough to spend time with these words and getting to know them, so they have deeper meaning and impact on your life and purpose. It's about loving yourself enough to know that you no longer have to stifle your desire to be more, because God has already said you are. It's about loving yourself enough to know that you are worthy and capable of living the life you want, if you're willing to put in the time.

Affirmations are the first step to manifesting your life goals because you're actually affirming what you bring to the table. It starts the process of building trust within yourself and the Spirit that lives in you. This is love in action because it's about surrendering to your best self and replacing your doubts. Have you ever been in love? A love so deep that you get butterflies just thinking about that person, excited by the anticipation of your next interaction? Captivated by every word? Fascinated by the way they think? Drawn in by their reaction to your own depth? You're open. Willing. Ready to experience life with this person because you trust them because it feels as though they are an extension of your soul. Whew! Now, imagine if you felt that way about yourself.

Love creates a balance to hate. Trust creates a balance to doubt. Complete trust is when your thoughts, feelings and actions are aligned. Complete trust in yourself takes some serious work, especially if you're trying to overcome negative thoughts. Trusting is knowing and it cannot be silenced by negative opinions, including your own.

Affirmations put you in the state of knowing, which is a state of consciousness. This means that you have to wake up to your power. Basically, you need to stop sleeping on yourself, because you are EVERYTHING! God created us to be amazing creatures with complexities. One of those complexities is the human brain. There's a part of the brain called the Reticular Activating System (RAS) that allows the brain to filter instructions from your conscious mind to your subconscious mind. The key things to know about the RAS is that it can be programmed and it doesn't know the difference between real situations or made up scenarios.

Affirmations are important because they allow you to create a clear picture that goes directly to your brain. This visualization can be supported and enhanced with a physical vision board or narrative, which we will talk more about later. Here's the thing, if you see yourself through broken glass, your self-image is distorted and the vision is blurred. A blurred vision makes it hard to figure out what pieces go where. If you picture life as a puzzle, it's hard enough trying to put the pieces together. Imagine trying to put the same puzzle together with drunk goggles on, it's certainly going to be harder, if not impossible.

Here's the homework: Write positive affirmations for yourself and affirm yourself and the goals you have for your life. You can start with some of the scriptures, by making them personal. For example, "I know the Word of God to be true. I am wise because I put these words into action every day." Start thinking about ways that you can make these true in your reality. As a bonus, I have sprinkled simple affirmations throughout the book, to remind you that you are able to do your thing. Once you believe you can, you will.

God's Promise: "Then the Lord replied: "Write down the revelation and make it plain on tablets so that a herald may run with it. For the revelation awaits an appointed time; it speaks of the end and will not prove false. Though it linger, wait for it; it will certainly come and will not delay." – Habakkuk 2:2-3

Reimagine Your Life

Part of the affirmations work is deciding that you are indeed enough and worthy of the things you want to accomplish. This section is about deciding *what* it actually looks like to trust you, love you, and walk in your worthiness with visualization. We talked about how this process is set in motion by the act of writing your affirmations. Remember, at this point we are still working on the "How You See Yourself" circle of your personal brand. The step of reimagining your life takes intention and several iterations. It doesn't happen overnight and changes as you accomplish goals and your goals get bigger.

In order for this to be useful to you, you should think about your learning style and complete this step in the style that resonates most with you. This act of visualizing is just reorganizing the life narrative you already repeat to yourself every day. I will provide three ways to help you manifest your vision that try to accommodate different learning styles. But first, here's a quick lesson on different learning styles to see where you might fit and what might be the best technique to focus on.

Visual Learners learn through *seeing* things. Typically, they understand and like charts, need quiet study time, and have to think a while before understanding a lecture. Some learning suggestions for visual learners include:
- Make an outline.
- Take notes, make a list.
- Color code words.
- Use flashcards

Auditory Learners learn best through *hearing* things. Typically, they like to read to themselves out loud, follow spoken directions well, can't keep quiet for long periods. Some learning suggestions for auditory learners include:
- Use word association to remember facts.
- Record lectures.
- Tape notes after writing them.
- Use flashcards.

Kinesthetic Learners learn best through *experience and doing* things. Typically, they like to build models, study with loud music on, and can't sit still for long. Some learning suggestions for kinesthetic learners include:
- Role play.
- Study with others.
- Study in short blocks.
- Use flashcards to memorize.

Do any of these seem like you? You may even be a mix of them all, depending on the content. This is just a snapshot, so if you're interested in learning more about your style or other styles, feel free to do your own research. I have done visioning a few ways and they are all honestly very helpful. Here are the 3 type of vision exercises I have used:

- Create an actual vision board with a medium sized poster and magazines, printed pictures or your own creativity.
- Create a vision board using Pinterest.
- Write out a life narrative and read it out loud.

I think there are benefits to each of these methods and probably a reason that you can do all of them. One of the reasons why I like creating the physical vision board is because the process of pulling pictures, colors, and themes is organic. The drawback to the physical vision board is getting all the supplies together, unless you're going to a vision board party on someone else's dime. My problem has always been keeping them on display since I don't have workspace outside of my kitchen.

I really enjoy Pinterest for creating vision boards because it's curated content available for free. I also like the fact that the pictures link to helpful resources or more information about the topic. It can definitely be the wild west in terms of quality of content available but I like it because of the organizational aspect it offers. One additional resource that I have included is the WTF journal. The WTF Journal is organized into four categories: faith, family, focus, and finances...and simply asks "Where's the...? It's a helpful tool to even figure out *WTF* you want in your life and how to organize the narrative.

In the day-to-day it can be hard to remember the "why" behind the "what" especially when things get tough. As humans, we can be insular, unable to see how things relate to the big picture or anyone besides ourselves. That's why this visioning concept and process is so important. If you think back over tough times, you can see clearly the reason why you went through that situation because hindsight is always 20/20. In this process you must not lose your foresight – your reason, your why.

That's when the visual and audible cues become so important to remind you that there's a reason why you chose to go through this, especially when it seems too far off and you're losing courage and momentum. This is not to say that visioning will keep you steadfast 100 percent of the time. But you have to create the cues to encourage yourself as you work on yourself. You have to become your best advocate.

Even if you don't really like vision boards, I suggest working through a journal specific to your goals. I really like the WTF Journal (not because I put it together) but because it's also a mirror. My business coach reminds me of how important it is to have something or someone remind you of the things you say and do and making you aware of those things and helping you develop the tools you need to make those things a reality. Here's the homework: Complete a visioning activity that best resonates with your learning style. The visioning process is meant to be a mirror of your innermost desires, taking them from just simple ideas to your real life. It's not a reflection of what you don't have, it's an observation of this season. Does it match your ideal narrative? If not, it's time to do something about it.

BONUS WTF JOURNAL PAGES AT THE END

PIVOT with Intention

- Perspective leads to purpose
- Isolation is necessary for clarity
- Vet your ideas
- Outsmart your worst habit
- Tithe through your trauma

I believe that there are times when we put too much on God. Of course, there's nothing too great for Him to conquer, but He also says that we, ourselves are more than conquerors. We neglect to recognize the power of the Spirit that lives within us. God says that we were created in his image. The Bible tells us that the goal is to be more like Christ. So, it makes sense that if we have a relationship with Christ, we strive to be like Christ, then we are an extension of that Spirit, of that power. This means that we have the ability to manifest the things we pray for by intentionally evoking the Spirit (power) that is already within us.

This is a concept I learned more about from author Wayne Dyer's *Manifest Your Destiny*, a book I received from one of my mentors, Rosetta Thurman, founder of Happy Black Woman. This lesson is about how to really start to change your perspective and hone in on the direction you want to choose. It's time for you to pivot, with intention. Pivot as a noun is said to mean, "any thing or person on which something or someone functions or depends vitally." Everything in this lesson; perspective, people, ideas, habits, and tithing are all vitally dependent on you giving them meaning. You are at the center of your life. All things that happen to you, also require a certain response from you in order for it to have any significance. Not only are you the pivot point, but you are also at a time when you must pivot your direction in order to move from the place you are now. I can just see so many thoughts and ideas starting to bubble up and over in your mind. This part should be fun!

---✦---

God's Promise: "For I know the plans I have for you, declares the Lord, plans to prosper you and not to harm you, plans to give you hope and a future." – Jeremiah 29: 11

Perspective leads to purpose

I hope you're ready because this is the point where things are about to shift. You are ready to come up from the valley, climb your mountain and take in the view. You're ready for your perspective to change and embrace your purpose. Perspective is important, because we make our decisions based on how we view the world. The view is limited in the valley, but God can bring good out of seemingly impossible situations. The Spirit of God works through our circumstances and choices. These are opportunities for God to really give us perspective.

The Spirit has an eternal perspective, whereas we only have our humanly perspective, which can sometimes impair our long-term vision. Gaining a new perspective is about changing your viewpoint, which essentially is what the pivot does. This is when you have to make a decision that things will indeed be different. One of my favorite quotes is "She decided she could, so she did." It's time to decide how everything that has happened in your life up to this point has informed, molded and shaped your story and purpose. The dream is no longer deferred.

Making this shift in your perspective will allow you to see that not everything somebody thinks or says about you is really about you. Changing your lens gives you empathy, the ability to see and feel the needs of others. When you are able to heal and look beyond yourself, you can start to learn and listen to what other people's needs are. Once you listen, you can understand what role you can play in meeting those needs and making other people's lives better. Your intention behind making yourself better will start to influence everything and everybody around you, and if they aren't willing to support you and keep up, that's the universe telling you that it may be time to shift your circle as well.

The point now is to listen to what your life story has been telling you up to this point and think about what it has taught you. Then, change the angle and think about what it can teach your future self or someone else who might be struggling with something similar. It's hard to fathom that God would want to use "our story" to change the world, but he does. He has plans for us that we don't even have for ourselves and if he revealed it all to us at once, we would run because our perspective of what's possible is limited. With time and discipline, our perspective changes. What's keeping you in the valley? Time to reflect.

God's Promise: "Do not be deceived: bad company ruins good morals." – 1 Corinthians 15:33

Isolation is necessary for clarity

Some people can't stand to be alone because they associate alone time with loneliness. Loneliness scares people, especially if your happiness and worth is dependent on other people. Being alone affords you the opportunity to hear your inner monologue without distraction, which can be equally scary. How else will you remove your distractions and change some of your dialogue if you don't spend time listening?

Isolation is necessary for you to really gain clarity, especially if you are a creative type. In full transparency, this is me. Everything gives me a new idea. That means that no one idea is complete before I'm thinking about the next thing. This simply means, I effectively get nothing done. Unless, I'm conscious and aware of the most important things.

One task that was suggested to me and I actually did was about how to focus on a few things on your list. It was to make a list of 25 things you want to do or experience in your life. Then on a separate sheet of paper, write down the top 5 things from your master list. Then, focus on those things.

Do those 5 things correlate to your life goals? Probably. Consider the first 2 on your list. Could you focus on just those for a period of time? Sure. What is the actual goal of the top

2 on your list? Are there other steps that need to happen in order to make that "one" happen? More than likely, yes. Ok, so think about the things that need to happen to take this goal from just something on paper to actionable steps. I'm almost positive that there are several action items on the list.

You may begin to see that you have the start of an action plan, like we talked about in the "Eliminate Your Excuses" section. But none of this deeper thinking is possible without your ability to isolate for brief periods of time. Spending time with yourself should not scare you. Welcome the space to get to know yourself and love yourself deeper.

And here's another thing about isolation: you have to practice now. When you find yourself working tirelessly towards a goal that nobody else has, some people will start to fall back and question why you work so much or why they never see you anymore and why you are so this or that now. They'll start to judge you, not because you have changed, but because they haven't been able to make the changes they want for themselves.

Even Jesus spent time in isolation. And do you remember why he went to the wilderness? He went to the wilderness to fast and pray. I'm going to sidebar for a second: There's a reason why God sent us his son, not only to save us from ourselves but he sent us his son so that we could have a human experience to relate to. The Bible is full of stories of folks journeying to the wilderness in hopes of a test or an encounter that would lead to restoration. They had hope that their isolation would lead to greater insight. They found their strength in doing the will of the Lord and fulfilling their mission.

Writing this made me think of one of my favorite TV shows, *Naked and Afraid*. It's such a great show on Discovery Channel documenting what happens when you put two people together, naked in the elements, that have to survive for 21 days. Each person is allowed to bring one survival tool and they get a map of the terrain. They have to hunt and take shelter until the time comes when they have to journey out from the middle of the hell they are dropped in.

The show introduces the survivalists in video reels before the show, telling us what they're looking forward to and why they are participating. They are usually optimistic and excited going in and most of them want to test the skills they have learned in a real-life setting. They welcome the challenge. Throughout the show, the survivalists create video diaries and this is where the show really gets good because it shows their vulnerability and how the expectation of the actual challenge is different from the reality. Depending on the circumstances, they either find great strength throughout the process and finish the challenge or recognize their limitations within that situation and find the courage to know when enough is enough. No matter what the outcome, I always admire those people because I know that it could not be me. Even just applying for something like that is part of their mission to fulfill some aspect of their life goals.

I share this to say, it may not look and feel like you thought it would, but you get to decide what tools to use to get through tough times and accomplish your goal. And you also have a map. You may not know how to read the map or navigate the terrain right now, but that doesn't mean it's impossible. You too, have a mission to fulfill. Whether it be through personal, professional or spiritual goals. Sometimes, you need to walk alone, just to prove to yourself that you can.

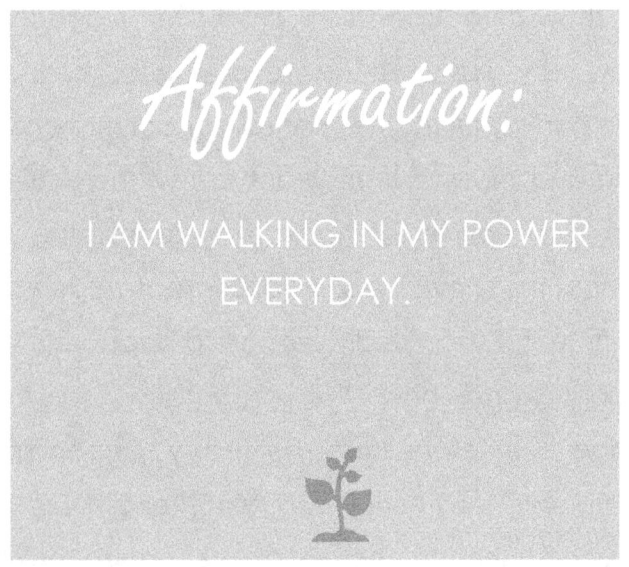

Affirmation:

I AM WALKING IN MY POWER EVERYDAY.

God's Promise: "As for you, always be sober-minded, endure suffering, do the work of an evangelist, fulfill your ministry." – 2 Timothy 4:5

Vet your ideas...and validate yourself

Starting something is not an accomplishment, although it's a monumental step. Starting is easy and has little value. To pivot your thinking and focus means rejecting the millions of other ideas that are not crucial right now. As a creative, I get how painful this sounds. But feeling overwhelmed and not being able to focus on one idea keeps you from fulfilling your ministry and sounds just as painful. I had to learn this. And the good news is that the creating doesn't stop. It happens in phases as you focus on different aspects of your big picture goals and ideas and you will build in that time as you learn more about routines, later. I think it's really important (and freeing) to be able to suffer through the process of vetting now because once you figure certain things out, you can apply the process to your other ideas.

You just have to consider one simple question when it comes to your many ideas: Is working on X going to get me to Y in Z timeframe? How you answer will tell you if that idea needs to be on your short-term or long-term list. Here's a simple idea that I read in an article by Steve Tobak titled "Make More Happen" in *Entrepreneur* magazine, "more is never better, better is better." With this thought, the author of the article reminds me of the power we put on money (or lack thereof) as a hindrance to accomplishing goals. If you're not already happy, money won't make you happy. If you're not already working on your goals or ideas, money won't make you start. You know why? Because you won't be prepared!

In my corporate career, I have worked on mostly grant funded projects, which means that I had to write a proposal every year and a half for my salary. In said proposal, the funder usually wants to know what you plan to do, how you plan to do it, how you came to the conclusion, and how much it will cost. And a lot of funders want to see that you already have the capacity to do the work, meaning that you can hit the ground running when the proposal is approved, even if you haven't received any money yet. Grants are great because they are often a mix between improving what you're already doing and planning a trip to the land of Oz. Even on the Oz end of things, where we don't always have everything figured out, we have to show that there are systems in place to support the work or a plan to create those systems.

To overuse the grant example, they are full of activities you hope to achieve over a given period of time, but related to one common goal. Not to oversimplify, but the major focus in my previous work was tobacco control. The main focus of my work now is childhood obesity and my personal work is about helping people overcome fear on purpose. There are several inputs (time, focus, money) and outputs (products, newsletters, services) that are underpinned by that common agenda.

The point is...you won't be able to write and publish your book, if you don't write your blog (preaching to myself and maybe you too)! You won't be able to accomplish your major life goals if you don't focus on one area and the small goals along the way. Even if your goal is to do several things, find comfort in the fact that you don't have to do it all at once or by yourself. One of the things I have learned from listening to and watching my mentors is that, once you do the hard, messy and tiresome work to figure out a system that works, you can replicate and modify over time. You won't get to this point if you don't vet your list and then validate what you choose.

Rosetta Thurman calls it the Chinese pizza in her teaching. She talks about a time when she went to a Chinese restaurant and they had a pizza station and a soul food station and probably some other types of cuisine, in hopes to appeal to the masses. In doing so, the thing that she went there to experience, their Chinese food, wasn't even all that. She tells this story to help her clients realize the power of being good at the "thing" they do that brings value to the community they want to build and serve.

I struggled with this in trying to find my "thing." Before my husband and I were married, we talked about all sorts of ways that we could make extra money by working for ourselves. We both had an inkling for having our own, but weren't quite ready to put in the time and energy into growing a business from the ground up. And hell, frankly, we didn't have the knowledge, even with us both having degrees. There are levels to this!

But, one day my husband jokingly said, I don't care if we run errands for older people that can't really get out. And I was on board thinking that it was a great idea, especially in the small community we were living in. So, we did all this work to file business paper work at the local and state level. We bought a website and hired a web designer. We had all of these promotional materials designed and printed. We even got a landline to feel official from our "home office." Yes, a landline.

Then one day, he came home and dropped the bomb that he didn't really think this was our "thing." Even though I was upset that we had invested time and money, I knew he was right. So, I moved on and we decided to pursue other things. I even decided that I wanted to start an online jewelry story. That was also a failure. This was all part of me running from the thing that I knew I should be putting my energy in to. It wasn't until I got fiercely clear and validated the fact that I was worthy and capable of doing my "thing" that I was able to make progress that I was happy with.

Are there examples of diverse business portfolios out there? Absolutely, but again, look at the time that it has taken. One example is Tyra Banks. Her business is beauty. She started as a model, expanded into TV with several shows and launched her own beauty line, but do you know what venture did not inherently fit in the model? Although extremely successful, Tyra's TV show did not fit and my guess is it was probably taking a lot of time from her other business goals that are her core. Tyra Banks is an amazing business woman that's been in the beauty industry forever and learned where her passions (and the money) collided. She wasn't afraid to let something go for the sake of the big picture.

And that's the part that will feel hard and uncomfortable at first, especially if you've already put some work or money into an idea. If it doesn't fit into the big picture goal or vision, it's probably not worth the time right now. Don't fear letting go, when holding on is doing more harm than good. Your time is your most valuable resource and you won't be able to make it back. There's no glory in being a Jack or Jill of all trades and the master of none.

There's quite a bit of homework for this lesson, because it's so crucial to moving forward with intention. There are several worksheets designed to help you get clear on what you bring to the table and how to cross walk that with a list of available options. The first part is to take inventory of your Strengths, Weaknesses, Opportunities, and Threats (SWOT analysis). A SWOT analysis is a tool used to assess internal and external factors to help make a decision. SWOTs are used a lot in strategic planning work for businesses when it's time to *pivot*.

The second part is to take inventory of your Passion, Product, People and Process, what I'm calling the PUSH analysis. The PUSH analysis is going to help you see where the **Passion** lies, **Understand** the money opportunities (products), figuring out who to **Sell** it to (people), and working through the **How** of it all (process). There are 4 key questions you need to answer to get through the worksheets. After you have completed both boxes with a level of detail you are comfortable with, you can then start to crosswalk your strengths with your passions and start planning for areas that you might be looking for additional training and resources, which we will talk about later.

Again, I know there is a lot of work during this section, but it's been designed to be intentional and to show you the processes I have gone through or go through as I continue to build my own brand and accomplish other goals as well. Part of the struggle of reaching our goals is our resistance to the focus it takes to get clear on what the heck we are even doing. Remember that God is not an author of confusion. Eliminating confusion depends on your ability to elevate your level of focus.

Bonus Promise: "For God is not a God if disorder but of peace – as in all the congregations of the Lord's people." – 1 Corinthians 14:33

Vet and Validate Worksheet – Part 1

Key Questions:

1) **Strengths**: What are the things you KNOW you are inherently good at?
2) **Weaknesses**: What are the things you KNOW you could improve on?
3) **Opportunities**: If given the opportunities, what would you like to work on related to yourself that would help you accomplish your goal?
4) **Threats**: What do you perceive to be the biggest threats to your success?

Strengths/Skills	Weaknesses
•	•
•	•
•	•
•	•
Opportunities	**Threats**
•	•
•	•
•	•
•	•

Vet and Validate Worksheet – Part 2

Key Questions:

5) **Passion:** What are the things you could/would do every day for free?
6) **Products**: What products or services can you create related to your passion that you can get paid for?
7) **People**: Who would be your ideal client/audience for those products and services?
8) **Process**: Who does what you want to do? What systems do they have in place that you can learn from about the process?

Passion	Products
• • • •	• • • •
People	**Process**
• • • •	• • • •

God's Promise: "No temptation has overtaken you that is not common to man. God is faithful, and he will not let you be tempted beyond your ability, but with the temptation he will also provide the way of escape, that you may be able to endure it." – 1 Corinthians 10:13

Outsmart Your Worst Habit

We are slaves to whatever has mastered us. Are you a slave to your bad habits? I know I have some habits I could stand to outsmart...Are you building habits around fear? Remember when we talked about fear causing paralysis, as a brain response to your conditioning? No? Well, to put it simply, fear creates bad habits, to the point where your brain no longer has to consciously think about it.

On their own, habits aren't very meaningful at all. But, over time, every good or bad habit impacts an outcome, such as health, productivity, and happiness. If you get up and go to the gym on a regular basis, you will yield results. If you focus on your project for even a few minutes on regular basis, you will yield results. On the same hand, if you never work on your project, you will yield those results as well. I started learning about habits as a part of a strategy team in my tobacco control job. One of the benefits of being a part of the group was a book read. One of our books was *The Power of Habit* by Charles Duhigg. His book "revolves around a central argument: Habits can be changed, if we understand how they work."

Duhigg "focuses on habits as they are technically defined: the choices that all of us deliberately make at some point, and then stop thinking about but continue doing, often every day." I agree that a better understanding of how such a process happens gives us the ability to rebuild those patterns in a way that we choose and has a more meaningful impact on our lives.

There's nothing you can't do if you get the habits right. There's been books written about the habits that can make a person more effective and successful, suggesting that there are a few common things that people can do *consistently* to reach and maintain certain levels of effectiveness and accomplishment. It's not easy or quick!

Bonus Promise: "The race is not given to the swift nor the strong but he who endures to the end." – Ecclesiastes 9:11

I want to transition for a moment just to talk a little bit about how habits work. Deep inside the brain are where our more primitive structures reside, controlling our automatic behaviors. You know this, but this has been studied with lab mice in mazes…overtime they take no time at all to find the cheese.

When scientists studied their brain function, they learned that the more they did it, the less brain power it took. When the brain converts a sequence of actions into automated routines, it's called "chunking." This "chunking" creates what Duhigg refers to as the habit loop, where the cue is presented, routine is created, and reward is offered. Routines can be physical, mental or emotional.

Habits are the foundation for how we behave, but the brain can't tell the difference between a good habit or a bad one. Old habits always remain inside your head, which makes them hard to break! It's much easier for the brain to revert than revise. Fortunately, habits aren't destiny, if you don't want them to be.

Did you know that even as late as the 1900s, most Americans didn't brush their teeth? That made selling the earliest version of toothpaste problematic for its investors. Thanks to ad man, Claude Hopkins, toothpaste is a national treasure, and halitosis is a choice. Hopkins' success came from being able to manufacture a cue that would cause a need for a particular product to be used regularly, thus creating a habit. He only had two steps: 1) find a simple and obvious cue and 2) clearly define the rewards.

Successful people are able to determine these in their plans and create habits around them because they are able to create a craving for the reward. What do you crave enough to reach your life goals?

God's Promise: "The point in this: the one who sows sparingly will also reap sparingly, and the one who sows bountifully will also reap bountifully." – 2 Corinthians 9:6

Tithe through your trauma

This isn't a lesson so much about why you should tithe, but more so, how you can tithe with and through the trauma life has given you. I remember first hearing Dr. Venus Opal Reese talk about the importance of tithing as a strategy to moving forward. She shares that whenever she is feeling extremely tight or pressed, especially when it comes to money, it's a trigger to give. This is a concept she learned she had to work through because of her past and the relationship that so many of us have with money. We learn to live with a lacking and longing heart, so we feel so connected to the money that we do have that we aren't willing to plant in the right season.

Tithing doesn't always mean money, although that biblical principle is important. Society has taught us that money is the only measure of success, worth giving. I get it. It's the currency of the times, but currency doesn't always mean relevancy. Don't you know that you have so much more to offer than money?

*Bonus Promise: "We have different gifts, according to the grace given to each of us. If your gift is prophesying, then prophesy in accordance to your faith; if it is serving, then serve; if it is teaching, then teach; if it is to encourage, then give encouragement; if it is giving, then give generously; if it is to lead, do it diligently; if it is to show mercy, do it cheerfully." – Romans 12:6-8

What a mighty promise from God. Not only does he give you gifts because of grace, but he says that you can do those things well and they are pleasing in his sight. Tithing is an act of sacrifice that shows obedience and trust in the Lord. I think you should also trust the Lord with your life goals. Trust him enough to know that your gifts and talents are enough to make a difference to someone, somewhere. Don't be so hidden in your darkness that you ignore your ability to pivot from this place and use it to elevate your purpose. There are 3 ways I believe that you can tithe without money:

1.) **Time** – Time is a big excuse we use to avoid certain things. Consider giving your time to meaningful causes that bring honor and dignity to someone other than yourself.

2.) **Treasures** – We live is a society that is driven by consumerism. If you're not already consumed with stuff, you're looking for stuff to be consumed with. In the next section, I'm going to talk more about making room for "newness" in your life, in ways that don't take up physical space. If you have a bunch of "trash" that could serve as a "treasure" to someone else, give it away.

3.) **Talents** – Like God has said, we all have many talents and gifts. I want to challenge you to donate your trauma. Not as a means to bond in misery, but as a way to minister to others. This is process that can be therapeutic for you and inspirational to someone else that needs to know, trouble don't last always. Giving your tenths matter and it should not be replaced, but giving of yourself is what matters to building and uplifting God's kingdom.

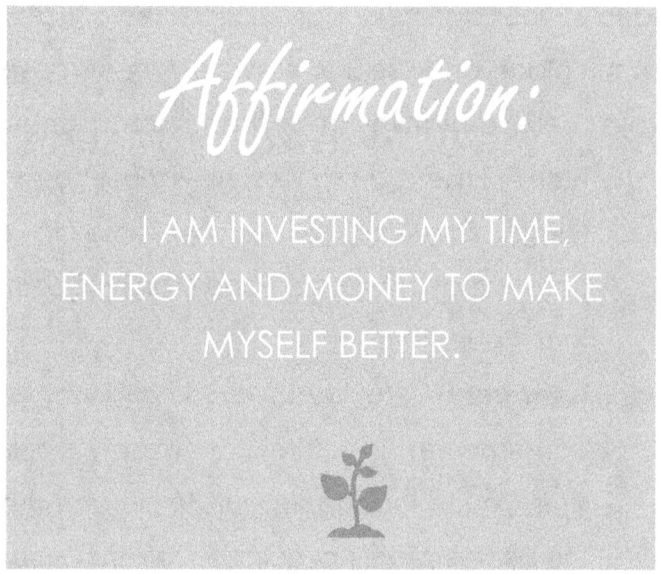

Affirmation:

I AM INVESTING MY TIME, ENERGY AND MONEY TO MAKE MYSELF BETTER.

Create SPACE for God

- **S**tudy your instructions
- **P**ray for discernment
- **A**llow yourself to feel the dispair
- **C**lean your physical space
- **E**xert the right energy

Pour into me...Is this your prayer? It's good to give yourself time to reflect...and be reminded that it's okay to not feel okay some days. To be honest, there will be days that you might feel completely empty. NO words to encourage yourself, let alone be what you need to be to everybody else. I remember a time when I was asking and praying for God to pour into me. Give me the strength I need to make it through another day. Then Beyoncé dropped her *Lemonade* album.

This is where and when I allowed myself to become unglued and listen to her visualize the beauty, pain, and angst of being a woman, especially a black woman. It took me through a range of emotions that I just had to release. She goes through ALL the emotions we feel when any meaningful relationship disappoints us. Even the relationship we have with ourselves.

She takes us through intuition, denial, anger, apathy, accountability, transformation, forgiveness, emptiness, and lastly, hope! And because of this my emptiness stopped feeling like the burden it once did. It started to feel like a beacon of hope, to be able to pour out once again. It allowed me to know that life is a journey and God needs you to feel some of these ugly things so you can really experience and appreciate the magnitude of the transition that occurs when you decide to change.

After you do this work to pivot and shift your perspective, you're going to need to do some work to build up your emotional wellbeing. This is your capacity to be able see your emotions and the emotions of others for what they are and act accordingly. This section is about handling the emotional and spiritual warfare that will surely come as you get closer to walking in your purpose-driven walk and presenting your new brand (YOU!) to the world. We talked about fear just being an emotion. And emotions are just feelings, not facts.

We're going to talk mainly about the feeling of despair and how you push through it with prayer. This work is just as much about faith, as it is about focus. I told you this was a journey about self-love and trusting yourself. You have to have faith not only in yourself, but in the Spirit and power of God that lives inside of you. But you won't believe that you have that power if you don't know what it looks and feels like. You have to get to know yourself and see yourself as God sees you, by giving Him the space to move. The belief that "God is..." and "I can't" can't exist in the same space, without one becoming more dominant than the other. This type of incongruent thinking will continue to keep you from living out your purpose.

The question is, are you empty enough to let God flow to and through you? There's nothing wrong with being in despair looking for a word from the Father. You need to allow God to move in your sacred space, making room for HIM. This lesson is about building and expanding your prayer life. Prayer is an invitation for God to come into your space so that the Spirit can speak encouragement and clarity into your life.

---- ✦ ----

God's Promise: "Keep this Book of the Law always on your lips: meditate on it day and night, so that you may be careful to do everything written in it. Then you will be prosperous and successful." – Joshua 1:8

Study God's Instructions

To evoke God's wisdom and instruction, you have to start by creating some space between the things and people you KNOW are posing as a distraction to your process. It doesn't even have to be a long time. When I wrote the original content for this lesson on my blog, I was sitting in the car by myself as it rained and thundered for about an hour and a half. As I cried my tears along with the heavens, God said "You are loved." Even when you don't feel it. It may seem like things won't go on if you're not paying attention to them. But they will.

Why was there such a gap between my actual feelings, when I know that God loves me? First, we can't experience God in the flesh, so it's harder for us to imagine that there is a force that loves us beyond what the world has to offer. Secondly, God wasn't embedded in my mental narrative because I hadn't spent time with the love notes he provided in his Word. I'm terrible at Bible study, but as I learn and grow, I'm trying to figure out methods that work for me to make things habit. This is a process I'm still working on but I wanted to offer some methods and steps for increasing the effectiveness of your Bible study time.

I'm always envious of people that can just pull out scriptures or stories for any given situation. I know that just may not be my ministry or yours, but I started thinking about it and realized they could do such things because they studied. Knowing his words means knowing him. As I looked for ways to be more intentional, I came across a few methods that are simple enough; you're probably already doing at least one of them. I found that I do the SOAP method during church services and the GROW method during my own time. This is not an overnight process, just like when you pick up any new topic, you have to spend time and ask questions and go back over it again.

Need some thoughts on where to start? You can either study by topics or books in the Bible. It's suggested that you read between 10-12 verses of a chapter and focus your study on those words. This approach may be different if you are doing topical study, where there may be several verses from all over the Bible, but you can still use that same idea by collecting 10-12 scriptures and using the method that best resonates with you. There is no wrong way to approach this if you are intentional about giving God your time. The next few pages are structured approaches to studying the Bible.

GROW Scripture Study

You're invited!

Greet: Invite God into your quiet time by opening in prayer.

Read: Read the verse silently or out loud a few times.

Observe: What stood out to you as you read this verse?

Write: Write out the verse, your observations and a prayer.

SOAP Bible Study Method

Scripture: Write out one verse that was meaningful to you.

Observation: What was interesting in this passage? What did you learn? What was God saying to you?

Application: How can you apply this scripture to your life? How will you let it change you?

Prayer: Respond to God in prayer, use the scripture as a guide. Ask God to help you meditate and apply the scripture to your life.

Swedish Bible Study Method

A light bulb: This should be something that 'shines' from the passage – whatever impacts most, or draws attention.

A question mark: Anything that is difficult to understand in the text, or a question you would like to ask the writer of the passage or the Lord.

An arrow: A personal application for your life.

God's Promise: "Therefore I tell you, whatever you ask for in prayer, believe that you have received it, and it will be yours." – Mark 11:24

Pray for Discernment

There are times when I don't even know the words to pray. Do you ever feel like that? I have learned that my first prayer should always be for God to help me be STILL enough so I can hear Him when he speaks. Because He will. Do you know that you fulfilling your purpose is a part of God's plan to be exalted? God needs you to get to the business of being you so that when people see you, they see Him and become curious about this aura you have about yourself.

Somebody needs your message but the Enemy, manifested in your thoughts, has convinced you that you aren't worthy of sharing your gifts and talents with those they need them. Those thoughts will have you convinced that there is someone better than you to do what you have been called to do. You have already felt like your back is against the wall long enough. Now, the only choice is to walk forward, through the circumstance, even if you don't know where to start or what to do.

We are encouraged to take our burdens to the Lord, but the Lord also instructs us to seek him for guidance and that should always be your prayer. God does not create confusion, so if you don't know the words to say, just ask God for discernment, so that you can clearly decide which way you should go. Are you interested in learning more about how to pray? God tells us how to pray in Matthew Chapter 6, saying:

> "And when you pray, do not be like the hypocrites, for they love to pray standing in the synagogues and on the street corners to be seen by others. Truly I tell you, they have received their reward in full. But when you pray, go into your room, close the door and pray to your Father, who is unseen. Then your Father, who sees what is done in secret, will reward you. And when you pray, do not keep on babbling like pagans, for they think they will be heard because of their many words. Do not be like them, for your Father knows what you need before you ask him. This, then, is how you should pray: 'Our Father in heaven, hallowed be your name, your kingdom come, your will be done, on earth as it is in heaven. Give us today our daily bread. And forgive us our debts, as we also have forgiven our debtors. And lead us not into temptation, but deliver us from the evil one. For yours is the kingdom and the power and the glory forever. Amen."

Prayer is really just a conversation with God, and he doesn't need you to be long-winded (contrary to Deacon Board bylaws). But as with any conversation, I think it's ok to have a plan. I know you rehearse conversations, too! Of course, we make plans and God does what he does, but if you are new to trying to build a prayer life, I want to offer you some direction on the construct of simple prayers.

ACTS Method

Adoration: Give God praise and honor for who he is as Lord over all.

Confession: Honestly deal with the sin in your prayer life.

Thanks

Thanksgiving: Verbalize what you're grateful for in your life and in the world around you.

Supplication: Pray for the needs of others and yourself.

God's Promise: "The Lord is close to the brokenhearted and saves those who are crushed in spirit. The righteous person may have many troubles, but the Lord delivers him from them all..." – Psalm 34: 18-19

Allow yourself to feel the despair

Through desperation comes breakthroughs. Despair is what pushes you so far to the brink of hopelessness that you have no choice but to claw your way out. This is when your fight or flight instincts will kick in...and you have to decide to fight. Despair creates that longing for change. When you long for something, you tend to maintain extreme focus on it.

Despair robs you of your hope in the moment, but if you allow God to use it, it's what's going to turn your burden into your beacon of hope. You have a choice in the matter. You can address what your despair is about and choose hope to light your path from darkness. You can choose fear itself or fear of the Lord. Remember that suffering is meant to propel you, not plummet you in the ground, causing you to lose sight of your worth. We have to be careful not to hold on to our suffering for too long though. For African Americans, suffering and surviving was all we had for so long. We've been so chained to that narrative, that we continue to accept it and pass it on. You are the one that can change that narrative.

To be real, despair does have its benefits because it will push you so close to your bottom that you will have no choice but to get up or give up. Despair will allow you to heal because a lot of those "excuses" are rooted in hurt based on what somebody in the flesh has convinced you is true. Your truth is rooted in something greater. Despair will have you asking questions and if you keep asking the right questions, solutions will start to rise to the top. The power of despair lies not in holding on to the feelings but remembering how to climb out. God wants you to be abundant not a blundering mess!

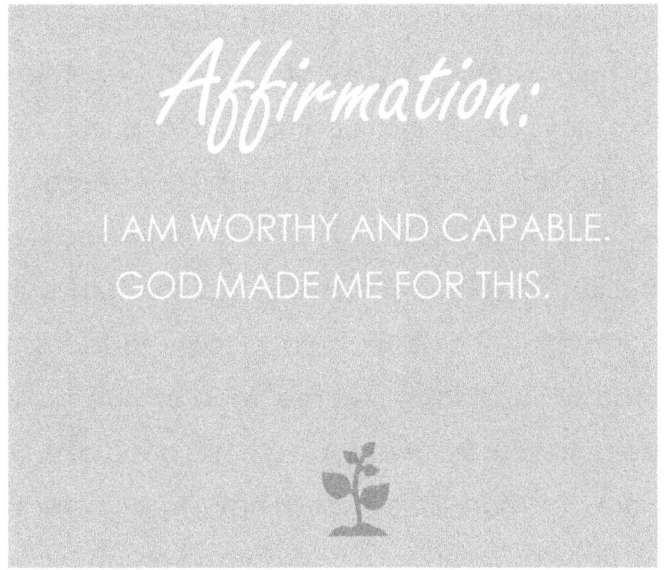

Affirmation:

I AM WORTHY AND CAPABLE.
GOD MADE ME FOR THIS.

God's Promise: "Then he said to them, 'Watch out! Be on your guard against all kinds of greed; life does not consist in an abundance of possessions." – Luke 12:15

Clean your physical space

These thoughts are really two-fold, you may actually have to create a physical space for you to unplug and check-in with yourself and the Spirit. If you don't have that possibility, it may be a matter of cleaning the space that you do have and getting rid of all that crap that is annoying you. A lot of the time, it's external clutter that is causing you all the extra internal noise.

The process of cleaning and de-cluttering has been known to provide many mental health benefits. From the physical movements to the completion of a task, people find cleaning cathartic. It's a great way to release frustration, anxiety, and anger to quiet your mind and welcome the truth. And the truth is, you don't need all that shit. That clutter serves as a distraction that effects your ability to focus. We have been fooled into thinking we are good at multi-tasking. I hate to break it to you, but even you are not good at it. None of us really are. Are there times when I have to do several things at once? Yes, absolutely, but that doesn't mean that someone doesn't end-up with the wrong shoe or better yet, no shoes (and an hour away from the house)!

You have to learn to choose quality over quantity. I was taught this lesson through a dietician friend, using chocolate. I'm not really a chocolate person, but I have an insatiable sweet tooth. My dietician friend helped me to understand that quality is going to keep you from going overboard in the quantity department. She told me that the darker the chocolate, the better it is and you won't overeat and you will satisfy your sweet tooth. Anyhow, I tried it and found it to be true. And the same goes with stuff, if you have the stuff that really matters, you won't need to overcompensate.

Think about what your clutter represents, because it may be deeper than you think. Are you hiding something or avoiding something? Are you using your cluttered space as an excuse? If you want to mediate and spend time with yourself and every time you look around, you feel overwhelmed by the amount of stuff in your way or lack of space, meditation then seems impossible. You will continue to be in a cycle of "blah". So, you may be thinking all this is great but where's the how and where do I start? Well, here are 5 easy tips to tackle your clutter.

Tackle Clutter Right Away:

1) **Bite off a small chunk at a time**. Set your timer on your phone for 20-30 minutes and get to work. When the timer is up, you're done, unless you want to keep going. Can you manage 20-30 minutes? Of course.
2) **Digitize your paperwork**. I'm a paperwork hoarder so I get it, you don't want to throw things away. But with

technology, almost everything can be digital now, so think about moving your paperwork to a digital format. And always back it up, if it's really important.

3) **Do you have valuables?** Sell them! If you have things that have even a little value that you're not using, why not try to unload?

4) **Keep a Sentimental Box.** I know there are some things you can't fathom parting with right now. I would suggest getting a sentimental box that includes some of your most treasured mementos, but be selective. Remember, quality over quantity.

5) **Get a collapsible file folder.** There are some things that you will need to have physical copies of paperwork for the process of adulting (i.e. birth certificates, marriage licenses, passports, etc.). I have a collapsible file folder where I try to keep all these documents, where I at least know that are in one place and somewhat easy to find.

Don't be afraid to let go of the things that are taking up the space for your newness. I have provided an easy checklist of ***BONUS: 50 Things to Throw Away*** at the end.

God's Promise: "I am the vine; you are the branches. If you remain in me and I in you, you will bear much fruit; apart from me you can do nothing." – John 15:5

Exert the right energy

I once heard Hey Fran Hey, from *The Friend Zone* podcast say, "Wherever attention goes, energy flows." This got me thinking about how intentional I was being with my spiritual journey. Was I spending enough time feeding myself spiritually? When I examined myself, I learned that when I felt disconnected from myself and out of control of the things around me, I also was feeling disconnected from the Spirit that lives within me.

There's a passage from Wayne Dyer's book that really resonated with me about energy. He says, "There is absolutely no difference in the power that brings anything from the world of waves into the world of particles, and the power that brings your thoughts or mental pictures into form." If you think about it, that power can be the Spirit, in whatever form you believe it to be. We often see ourselves as separate from the power that makes things happen, even though we a part of the story that makes the power what it is. The power has no purpose if you don't believe it will work. The power has no purpose if you don't give it energy.

Have you ever walked into a room and felt that the life was just sucked out of you? Have you ever been in a room and when a person walks in, it just brightens up? You're experiencing the energy of other people, which should tell you just how strong your own energy can be. What's your energy like? Do you dwell on the negative? Do you accept things that you know you can change as unchangeable? All of those decisions are a signal to the universe that you may not really want change. Or you're unwilling to accept your responsibility for making it happen.

Giving your energy to the wrong person and things will cause a shortage for the things that actually deserve it. You only have so much to give and you have to respect that. I understand that it's not always easy to manage your energy, but you can learn to get better at what you are actually putting out in the universe and examining what's manifesting around you. Does it line up? If so, that should be proof that if you exert more positive energy through thought and action, then more positive things will also manifest in your life.

Words are energy that have the ability to create. Remember how God created the earth, moon and stars? He spoke those things into existence. And God has the ability to move suddenly, so when opportunities arise, that you have been believing and expecting, that's an indicator that it's the right time to move in that direction.

SPARK Your Higher Self

- Set your intention
- Plan for the pressure
- Align with like-minded people
- Revamp your routines
- Keep pushing yourself

I believe that your purpose has already been predetermined. I also believe that you have the ability to support your purpose through thoughts and action. You can transcend the limitation of the world that tells you you're not good enough, you're not ready or you don't have what you need to move forward. You have to be willing to participate with assurance in the act of creation. You have to be willing to loosen your emotional attachment to what you view as your reality. Some of this starts with the SPACE work, which will continue throughout the rest of your time, but hopefully that work brings you more clarity. And that clarity should give you the confidence you need to SPARK the higher version of yourself. I don't take it lightly, because I know this is hard and ongoing. I want to be clear, once again, that it doesn't require perfection. I refuse to let that be your hang-up. You know how I talked about my favorite show *Naked and Afraid*? Everyone that goes on that show knows that the first things they need to do is find water, build shelter, and start a fire. In fact, most bring with them a fire starting tool because they know just how important fire is to their survival. It can be used to keep them warm, send smoke signals, sanitize water and cook food, if they catch it. A lot of times, the fire starting process doesn't go as planned. They struggle because they have to put their skills to the test in a situation where it really counts. They start to realize that the skills and technique doesn't have to be perfect, as long as they can get a small spark to light the brush that can start the actual fire. The same goes for you. You don't need the perfect idea or to understand all there is to know to get started. All you need is the intention to move forward with the transition you're about to make. Doing the work in this chapter is meant to be that spark. In this chapter, we're talking about setting your intention towards success, taking care of yourself in the process, the importance of like-minded people and routines, as well as encouraging yourself to push through to the next level.

God's Promise: "…But one thing I do: Forgetting what is behind and straining toward what is ahead, I press on toward the goal to win the prize for which God has called me heavenward in Christ Jesus." – Philippians 3: 13-14

Set your intention

Are you ready to define your goal(s)? Or even take it a step further and define your *why* for this particular goal? How do you become more intentional? Recall your life narrative, recall why you thought this book would be a good read for you. We have already been talking about intention, but it's time to get serious about the specifics. Being intentional about goals starts with being clear and writing it down.

Intention is the starting point of accomplishing your life goals. Intention starts with you first becoming aware and doing the work it takes for your desires to be congruent with your actions. This work begins with the awareness of self and what those desires are. You are well on your way to all the foundational work that helps in being more intentional with your life. Your intentions assist you in taking the control that is necessary to manifest what is already yours.

Intention simply defined means "to have in mind a purpose or plan, to direct the mind, to aim." Aligning your thoughts and actions when you actually put a plan together and work that plan, opens the door for the universe to be the Scottie Pippen to your Michael Jordan.

Here's where I want to talk more about SMART goals and really define them and give some examples:

Specific: state exactly what you want to achieve. Can you break a larger task down into smaller items? Remember that intention is about being clear about what you want. The first step in a smart goal is about being specific about what exactly you want to achieve. Saying that you want to start a business or a blog or change your career path is not specific enough. What kind of business? What do you want your blog to be about? What kind of career path do you want moving forward? We need to think about those details in this section. I'll use this book project as an example: I want to complete my first chapter book by August 31, 2016 by writing at least 350 words everyday starting April 1, 2016. In this example, the primary target is to write 350 words every day.

Measurable: establish clear definitions to help you measure if you are reaching your goals. Goals are measurable when you quantify them. When you know the progress you are making toward your goal, you stand the chance of meeting them faster. Continuing with the book example, I included the specific amount of words I needed to write every day in order to feel like I was on track with my goal. Also knowing the specifics of what I needed to do, helped me plan my writing times accordingly. If I had a day where I was traveling for work and couldn't do much, I would shift to using those days as research days so when I could write again, I would be prepared to write at least 700 words.

Action-oriented/attainable: describe your goals using action verbs, and outline the exact steps you will take to accomplish your goal. A goal is said to be attainable when its accomplishment is within reach. Do you have the skills and abilities to take action to reach your goal? Are you motivated? Are you prepared to take the action steps required to reach your goal? I set a goal for the book project to be done within four months. I believed that this was attainable, not only because I was willing and capable of doing the work, but also because I had a good starting point with all the work I had been doing prior through my blog content. I knew some practical next steps were to get organized by creating an outline; filling in the outline with content that was already started; then figuring out the huge gaps. From there I was able to plan tangible next steps.

Realistic: give yourself the opportunity to succeed by setting goals you're actually able to accomplish. Be sure to consider obstacles you may need to overcome. I believe that you can reach for the moon and the stars, but remember that this life is a journey and there is some practicality that goes along with goal achievement. We're going to start small and realistic, but we're not going to stay there! I believed my goal was realistic because I practiced through my blog and in the weeks leading up to my start day. When it came to obstacles, there were some that I knew would come up and then there were those that were completely unexpected. I have a family that includes a husband and children, one of which is a very active 2-year-old that doesn't care that mommy has goals. His goals are to be fed, played with and loved on. If you have some of these same factors competing for your time and attention, have the conversation with your support system to let them know so they can help you manage and find balance between all the things that matter. It also helps your family to manage their expectations of you.

Time-Bound: how much time do you have to complete the task? Decide exactly when you'll start and finish your goal. Goals must have specific time frames. If you determine how much time you will give yourself in days, weeks or months and have a specific date in mind, that will keep your goal in the forefront of your mind. Notice that I didn't mentioned years. You can have a goal that you want to accomplish within a year, but I would not suggest having a SMART goal that extends passed a year for accomplishment. That would be more of a life goal, that probably has several SMART goals within it to complete. The other reason that the time is important is because you don't want to give yourself too much time. Too much time allows you to get lazy and complacent with thinking that you have time. You'll continue to put things off that can easily be marked off your list. In my example, I have a start and finish date. I planned and gave myself some time to work up to April.

There is proven research that suggests those that write their goals are more likely to achieve them, because of the power of intentionality. Remain confident in the power of your desire and the power that guides you. Your higher self is supremely aware that all things (even seemingly bad things) are working for your good. Stand on that, even without being aware of the details. Focus on the steps it takes rather than the specific outcome because sometimes things don't look or feel like we thought they would. These should still be counted as accomplishments because they move us from the place we started, which really is the point of life anyway.

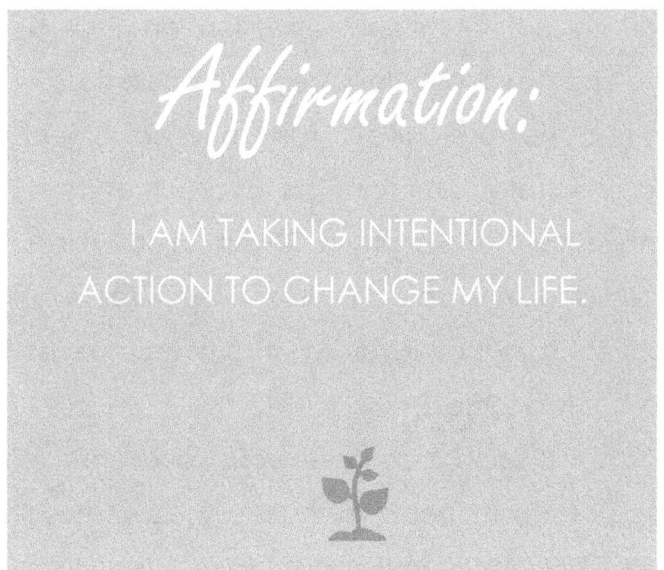

Affirmation:

I AM TAKING INTENTIONAL ACTION TO CHANGE MY LIFE.

God's Promise: "Be sober-minded, be watchful. Your adversary the devil prowls around like a roaring lion, seeking someone to devour." – 1 Peter 5:8

Plan for the Pressure (self-care)

As you go through the process of setting and accomplishing goals, shit gets tough. Mentally, emotionally, spiritually, and physically... depending on how much you are trying to accomplish within a given period of time. Any time you are trying to be better than good, resistance will flow to you. Remember when we talked about energy? Whenever you start to put intentional attention on your goals, an opposite energy will also flow, because of inertia.

Inertia is the resistance of any physical object to any change in its state of motion. This idea comes from Sir Isaac Newton's first two laws of physics: 1) An object at rest tends to stay at rest and 2) An object in motion tends to stay in motion. Basic physics says that, if you want to overcome inertia, you have to apply a force.

As you expand, change your direction, etcetera, resistance to that idea will naturally flow. Resistance is anything (including people and places) that slow or stop movement or keep movement from happening easily. I'm reminding you of this because I know you have already been through some type of hell and back! I know you've experienced a time when things were seemingly OK, then all of sudden things went to the left, to the left. I'm saying this to remind you that you made it through that. I need you to remember that and start thinking about the things that almost had you and take inventory of the things you did or said that got you through it. I'm talking about building up your resilience to the resistance. Resilience is this idea that the capacity in which we deal with our discomfort and adversity has the ability to enrich our lives tremendously and these skills can be learned.

There are several things that you can do to improve your resiliency, but I think that it all goes back to self-care. I've heard about self-care but as I started to work on myself and more of my goals, I started to realize the importance of this idea. Daily habits play a role in your ability to bounce back from set-backs, such as getting enough sleep, eating your pineapples (and other fruits and vegetables), and keeping your stress at bay. Regular mental breaks = Regular Self Care Routine. If you want more information about clear and concise steps of self-care, I'm recommending fellow Happy Black Woman tribe member, Aisha Moore of Self-care by Aisha. You can download her Self-care Planning Workbook at www.selfcarebyaisha.com. Aisha's work is about creating a plan that works for you, but do you need something to do right now or have no idea what things would help you take better care of yourself?

Here are 10 Quick & Simple Self-care Tips:

1. Drink some water.
2. Take a walk.
3. Take a nap.
4. Write in your journal.
5. Get a pedicure.
6. Turn on "Do Not Disturb" or block "that" person.
7. Take a deep breath.
8. Watch a funny movie.
9. Cry.
10. Go to your mirror and repeat, "Not today, Satan." And walk away like you mean it!

Bonus Promise: "Beloved, I pray that all may go well with you and that you may be in good health, as it goes well with your soul." – 3 John 1:2

God's Promise: "Iron sharpens iron, and one man sharpens another." – Proverbs 27:17

Align Yourself with Like-minded People

I really don't remember how or when I first came across Rosetta Thurman, but it all started with me looking for something to get me on track. On her website, HappyBlackWoman.com, she was offering a free life-mapping workbook, that I downloaded. I remember it being so helpful in helping me really think about EVERYTHING that I envisioned for my life. I was hooked. There was something about this woman that really drew me in.

I started receiving her emails of encouragement and announcing here courses and I always sort of perused them and kept it moving. Then, around the time that I stopped running from what I actually wanted to do, I received an email from Happy Black Woman, announcing her "How to Become a Public Speaker" program. And I decided that I should make it work with my budget, because even though I knew what I wanted to do, I knew that I had no idea how to go about really getting the business in order.

After investing in her program, I was given a bonus ticket to her live blogging event, which I did not attend. And time went on and on and I was still following and trying to figure things out. I completed the tasks from the program and made myself official. Fast forward several more months and I get another email about a bonus ticket to another live event. This time, it was the Launch Your Business Boot Camp.

This was an event I had heard about and seen advertised in the past, but ignored it. Saying I didn't have the money or the timing wasn't right for my schedule. EXCUSES! I couldn't ignore God any longer after I received several emails and a voicemail telling me that I had this BONUS TICKET to the event. And can you believe that I did not even call her support team back right away?! TRIPPIN'!

I was able to spend an intensive 3 days in Atlanta at the event! Rosetta is a woman that I admire and respect because she is walking her talk, using her story to empower women, and ultimately changing lives. I was able to meet other powerful women that will change the world one day. And there were women in the room that told me, I too will change this world.

I have aligned myself with amazing, dynamic and influential women who also happen to be getting PAID! And I mean *millionaire* money. And now, the woman that I have called my virtual mentor (in my head) has been a part of my reality. She saw my face. She heard my name. I decided to actively align myself with the right people that could help me, inspire me and encourage me to walk MY talk.

This reminded me of a blog post I wrote about upgrading your circle. This is not to say that you should completely abandon your friendships but it is for you to assess the value of the time you spend with people that aren't like-minded versus the time you spend with people that inspire you and push you. And you should consider how these relationships affect your personal brand, after all YOU are your brand. And you are the sum of your top 5 friends.

I was able to meet people and eat lunch with people from across the country, and even the globe. I was about to listen to stories of women that came from absolutely nothing and are now running profitable businesses. I was able to have a conversation with Dr. Venus Opal Reese, the black woman millionaire mentor. And the way she stands in her power had the room on fire! And to be in this atmosphere was just the spark I needed to know that I too can stand in my power. And I believe that for you too.

You see, God has already said "YES" to us to get everything we want and desire in life. He's just patiently waiting for us to say "YES" to our blessings and be willing to accept his answers. Sometimes the problem is that we don't believe in the power, worth and value that we bring to the table. And we end up spending so much time avoiding the very things that we say we want. And that my friends, is FEAR. Be intentional about aligning yourself with people that will encourage you to step over the line of fear, people that have stepped over the line again and again.

God's Promise: "No discipline seems pleasant at the time, but painful. Later on, however, it produces a harvest of righteousness and peace for those who have been trained by it." – Hebrews 12:11

Revamp Your Routines

How are you doing so far? If you need a break, take one. Otherwise, I'm about to talk about something that really annoys me... complaining about not having enough time for the things you say matter to you. By now, you already know that's a major excuse. You have the time you may just not being using it properly or spending on the wrong stuff. This was a major struggle for me when I decided that I needed to work towards a major life goal. I learned that I needed to get serious about my routines to create better habits. What I have learned about myself is that I need to be highly scheduled until new habits become automatic.

I learned from my mentor, Rosetta Thurman, that the most important routine she has that she feels contributes to her success, is a meaningful and inspiring morning routine. I have read this before and knew it was a common habit among successful people. But, I'm like the queen of not being a morning person. An inspirational morning routine is said to set the intention for your day, and remember this whole process is about taking intentional action.

Thankfully, there are also nighttime routines that successful people also participate in. So depending on your style, there are ways you can "bookend" your day for success with intention. There are three things that I feel have helped me either unwind from my day and remember the joy that I had or wind down from a productive day and give thanks for it coming to an end:

1) **Gratitude journaling** – Spend time thinking about the things that happened throughout the day, I write down the things that frustrated me. I don't want to dwell on those things, but it's important to give myself the space to get it out of my head, think about it and see if it was a little thing to just chock up to the day or if it's a big deal or pattern that I keep seeing. It's like a check point to see if I need to change my surroundings or my response. To that end, for every one thing that frustrated me, I find at least two things that I am grateful for or that made me happy during the day. It forces me to see that the good outweighs the bad and sets my intention for my prayer.

2) **Prayer** – Your devotion is supposed to be in secret, but I will share that there are two things I do to set my intention for prayer. I light a candle and sing a song called Welcome Holy Spirit or any other song that's on my mind and just let God know that I am ready to talk.

3) **To-do list (top 3 things)** – There are so many tips about how to be productive and get the most from your brain

power throughout your day. I am a list person and like to check things off my list. Sometimes, the list has a tendency to get out of hand from time to time. One tip that I have tried is writing the top three things that you want to accomplish that day.

The things I do as a part of my night routine to set myself up for a better day, could theoretically be done in the morning too. One thing that I will say is that your routine, should be a part of your self-care plan and creating systems that support you operating as your best self should be prioritize over following what a "success guru" says. If you are a morning person, try it in the morning. If you need a wind-down routine to help you sleep better, which sets you up for a good day, try it at night.

The best way to create a new routine is to practice. Start with a day or two and see how you feel. Reward yourself for doing something. Always try again. Remember those "WWJD" bracelets, inquiring about what Jesus would do in said situation? Well, let me say that God/Jesus/Spirit would show you some grace when you fall short. So, show yourself some grace as well. I'd like to share a short story about grace and this project because it segues perfectly into the next section.

I set a pretty intense goal for myself to get this book project done and made all these internal deadlines and checkpoints. As my deadline was drawing closer, I had to reconcile and tell my coach that it just wasn't going to happen. She did a really great thing for me by asking me how I felt about that. I just said I was coming to terms with it. But I was very discouraged. In a much later call with her, I realized that there was a lesson in me missing my deadline. It was grace. I had to learn how to show myself grace because I knew that God had convicted me to do this book project. I wouldn't be able to talk to you about it if I hadn't experienced it with one of the most important projects to tackle for my business. Once I thought about it and did some gratitude journaling, I knew that I was once again back on track and things would get done. God's grace is always sufficient. He will carry you, that's why a routine conversation with him is important.

God's Promise: "No, in all these things we are more than conquerors through him who loved us." – Romans 8:37

Keep Going/Pushing

Though it is a simple concept, it's one of the hardest and the most important. Just when you think things won't get any better, God will show up and show you just how mighty he is and just how strong you are. He has given you a vision and a purpose for your life that you may not even be able to comprehend fully yet, but keep going, keep pushing through. You are right on the verge of your breakthrough.

Remember when we talked about the fight or flight response? The idea implies that there's a choice between what we let destroy the dream or define the exact moment when the perspective shifts. No matter what, decide to use the fight or flight instincts to keep going. Everything you need, you already have. I once heard a preacher say that you use what you do have to manifest what you don't have.

The good news about all this is that you already know that challenges will come, and now you have some tools and resources to keep you going when you see the obstacles coming, or even when you don't see them coming. The difference between those that overcome and those that don't is the way they react and approach the challenges and the meaning they attach to those challenges.

You have the response-ability to kick you into action. I'd like to share a story about how this book almost didn't happen, in the middle of the writing process. I can tell you that as soon as I decided that I needed to get this off my heart, the Enemy marked me as a target. The closer I got to meeting my deadlines, the less I wanted to write or had the ability to focus on writing. Even with my blocked time, it seemed as though every time I had the intention to be productive, there was an opposite force at work! I got to the point where I hadn't even opened the file in about 2 weeks, in the last month of writing. The discouragement I felt about not reaching my goal was plaguing my mind. Even though at the time, I hadn't actually missed my deadline.

It was a call with my coach that helped me to do one simple thing a day over the three days that followed our conversation that made me realize this too was something that I needed to experience. During our conversation, I suddenly remembered the title of the book. I'm telling you I was so buried, I didn't even remember the title and didn't even know that I had once again found myself to actually be sinking, fighting and clawing and getting further and further away from the mission.

This conversation was God speaking directly to me to say, you have what you need. And what's funny is that I had just read 1 Corinthians 1:7-9 from The Message Bible that reads:

"Just think – you don't need a thing; you've got it all! All God's gifts are right in front of you as you wait expectantly for our Master

Jesus to arrive on the scene for the Finale. And not only that but God himself is right alongside to keep you steady and on track until things are all wrapped up by Jesus. God, who got you started in this spiritual adventure, shared with us the life of his Son and our Master Jesus. He will never give up on you. Never forget that."

And that's when my coach said, you know that you are literally writing the book on this, right? You should go back and read the words that you have written for other people and use them to encourage yourself to keep going and finish this task. Even though it felt like I was delayed, way off track and unlikely to meet my deadline, I made the decision to keep going. I decided to stand on God's promises for my life and the vision that he gave me and know that sometimes it's not all about what we plan, but what God plans for us. I learned to trust him through the process and that all things will work out how they are supposed to. That period was probably the biggest test of my faith because, not only was I under attack, but my family was as well and I questioned was this even the right thing for me to do.

I have to spend some real time using my own advice, by choosing isolation, choosing prayer, choosing silence so that I can hear God and use what he has already given me to move to the next level. I just want to share this story because I know this works! There are powerful forces working against every decision you make that brings you closer to your purpose and God getting glory. But always remember that there is a force within you that is greater, and you have to keep going.

**Bonus Promise*:* "For still the vision awaits its appointed time, it hastens to the end – it will not lie. If it seems slow, wait for it, it will surely come, it will not delay." – Habakkuk 2:3

BUILD Your Brand

- Baby Steps
- Use your time for your goals
- Invest in yourself
- Leverage your network
- Do the work

Branding is not marketing. Branding is telling the story and connecting with your community, that in turn become ambassadors for products and services. Personal branding is about packaging your own story in a way that positions you as the expert in a certain area, and who better to be an expert of your life than you. One of the tips that I continue to hear about personal branding is how important it is for you to be your authentic self and communicate that clearly and consistently. That's one of the reasons that I feel all this other leg work and working on "self" is so crucial before you try to manage how "others" perceive you.

With the understanding that your brand is a reflection of who you really are and presenting your authentic self, it should now make sense that in order to build a brand you love, you HAVE to love yourself first. The work prior to this point is about figuring out how you feel about yourself and what you really believe about yourself and the world around you. This section is about looking at your strengths and weaknesses, and molding them to influence not only how you respond to life, but how life responds to you.

God's Promise: "Whatever you do, work at it with all your heart, as working for the Lord, not for human masters..." – Colossians 3:23

Business over busyness

Do you suffer from compulsive busyness? Bouncing from activity to activity without any real sense of accomplishment? If yes, it's no wonder because we have been trained to think that the amount of work we are involved in, somehow gives us meaning. Busy is code for being successful and important. With busyness, comes sleep deprivation and stress. If you truly are overcommitted, it's time to focus. Feelings of being tired, overwhelmed, afraid, hurting, uninspired, stuck were probably not present when you were visualizing and writing your life narrative.

We're going to talk about time in a minute, but it's important to figure out if you're busy or bullshitting. It's time to get real, if you truly want to build a brand you love to live. Activities start out as innocent ways to get involved and expose yourself to new and different things. Over time they become what some well-meaning adult calls "resume' builders" that can be used to assess your ability to become another well-meaning adult. While I fully appreciate the sentiment behind exposure, I don't think there's enough guidance on how to transition out of things without feeling like you're letting someone down. We carry these habits into adulthood, especially the inability to say 'no' and focus on the things that make us better, and happier.

It sounds and feels selfish but it's not. It actually takes a great deal of wisdom to know exactly what you want in this season and to focus on those things that will make this time in your life, worthwhile to you. You are a work in progress, which means you don't have to be perfect to pursue what makes you tick. Once you accept the fact that this is a journey, you have to decide to take the first step in putting together your plan and accomplishing your life goals. I'd rather take baby steps than no steps. Making time in your day to work on your baby steps will energize you and add purpose and meaning to your day. You need to ask yourself, how can I be my most productive self throughout the day, week, month, and focus on building some habits around increasing your productivity.

Increasing your productivity is easier said than done, I know. But we can talk about some practical ways (7 to be exact) to eliminate distractions.

1.) **Start with the end in mind** – Be super clear on the goal or outcome and remember why it's so important to you to accomplish your goal.
2.) **Manage the expectations of others** – You really don't owe people anything, but if you have family and friends that might worry or demand your time as well, try to do your best to manage their expectations by telling them about your goal or project or whatever

you're working on, so they know that you're alive and working on your goals.

3.) **Set time frames that maximize your best brain waves** – This one is hard. For me, it may not be the ideal time for my brain waves but I do have set times in my calendar to work on certain things. That allows me to know that at that time, I'm supposed to be working on X and I can start to prepare myself for getting the most out of that time, even when I don't feel like it.

4.) **Take breaks** – Recall your self-care plan here. You need to take breaks to refresh your mind and body. And this helps with the burn out that can come from working tirelessly on a project. But you can also make your breaks productive. I think there is a time and place for mindless activities (i.e. Netflixing) but when you're in a productive mood, use the energy to be productive elsewhere. Maybe take a 15-minute break to fold laundry or go for a quick walk. You may get clarity on the thought you were stuck on, even if you don't, you've at least accomplished a break and one step closer to having all the laundry done.

5.) **Keep a notebook** for unrelated thoughts to get them out of your head – it's a fact that once you start working on something, there will be a million other ideas or distractions that come your way. Make your brain and yourself happier by making note of those things in a random thoughts and ideas notebook. This allows you to honor the thought and move on.

6.) **Focus on PDA** – not the touchy, feely kind. I'm talking about purpose-driven activities in this case. If it's not a task that will get you closer to the end-goal, you probably shouldn't waste your valuable time on it. Prioritize your activities based on this idea. Don't use your good brain wave time on things that can wait.

7.) **Don't quit until you're done**. Simple. Work on it until you finish it. I know it doesn't always feel so simple, but it is. If you go at it with intensity for the time period you set within those timeframes, you have a good chance of getting it done. And even if you don't get to work on it within certain timeframes and you miss your deadlines, keep working on it until it's done. It matters. It matters because accomplishments send positive signals to your brain and you need those to keep you moving forward with anything that you pursue in life.

God's Promise: "There is a time for everything, and a season for every activity under the heavens: a time to be born and a time to die, a time to plant and a time to uproot..." – Ecclesiastes 3:1-2

Use *your* time for *your* goals

You can no longer work for your boss for free. Remember that time is your most valuable resource and your time outside of your day-job should be used for your goals. Owning your time is one of the first steps you can take to work towards your own Independence Day and achieving your life goals. We celebrate Independence Day in this country to remind us of the perils this country went through to become an independent nation, no longer under England's control. Independent; meaning not influenced or controlled by others in matters of opinion, or conduct; not subject to another's authority or jurisdiction. Let's use this time to reflect on our personal independence. I want to pose the question: Who owns your time?

Think about how much time you give away for free, scrolling on social media, hanging out, binging on Netflix... Don't get me wrong, I think you can do whatever you want with your time and there's nothing wrong with wasting a little time. But as with everything else, there has to be balance. Even when you're going hard for your goals, you have to make time for self-care or you will burn out.

I just don't want you to run out of time thinking that you have more time. Your time is your most valuable asset in life. I don't want you to be under Fear's authority, making excuses for the things you should have done yesterday or last month, or even last year. I don't want another year to pass by and you wonder what happened. Excuses will rob you of your time. We already know that you can convince yourself that things are true, even if they aren't (self-talk). If you keep telling yourself that you don't have time, you won't and you will continue to [out of habit] give your time away for free, doing nothing that brings you closer to your goals.

There's a reason why time is talked about using terms such as "own" and "spend". Like I said, it's an asset, much like money. Wealthy people or people that are building wealth are good examples of this concept. A lot of wealthy people are rich, but not every rich person is wealthy. Let's go a little deeper. Wealthy people are able to create systems that free up their time while still making them money to support themselves and their lifestyle. Rich people have to continue to be workhorses because they don't want to spend the time to figure out how to create a system that runs without them.

Speaking of systems that run without the workhorse, this idea becomes critically important if you're thinking about goals that will sustain your family tree. Are you doing what it takes for your legacy to live on? Another characteristic that I have noticed about wealthy people or people working towards wealth is that they understand and appreciate delayed gratification as a part of the process. They know that when approaching a new project, not everything will work out perfectly the first time. In fact, from my experience it's more of the process of building something and seeing it through that's more enjoyable. We live in a world where everything is expected to yield instant results. We have become uncomfortable with "in due time", that's a phrase my grandma used to say to me all the time when I was younger. We have to learn that the Spirit has no time frame that we understand and to trust that process.

Are you working towards your own Independence Day, when you are no longer under the company's control, or the opinions of others? I encourage you to fight for your freedom, by being intentional. Be intentional with your thoughts, your energy, and your time. Here's the homework: Complete the time audit over a period of at least 3 days. Carve out at least 10 hours for yourself to work on you and your goals.

BONUS TIME AUDIT WORKSHEET AT THE END OF THE BOOK

God's Promise: "The Parable of the Bags of Gold" – Matthew 25:14-30

"Again, it will be like a man going on a journey, who called his servants and entrusted his wealth to them. To one he gave five bags of gold, to another two bags, and to another one bag, each according to his ability. Then he went on his journey.

The man who received five bags of gold went at once and put his money to work and gained five bags more. So also, the one with two bags of gold gained two more. But the man who had received one bag went off, dug a hole in the ground and hid his master's money.

After a long time the master of those servants returned and settled accounts with them. The man who had received five bags of gold brought the other five. 'Master,' he said, 'you entrusted me with five bags of gold. See, I have gained five more.' His master replied, 'Well done, good and faithful servant! You have been faithful with a few things; I will put you in charge of many things. Come and share your master's happiness!'

The man with two bags of gold also came. 'Master,' he said, 'you entrusted me with two bags of gold; see I have gained two more.' His master replied 'Well done, good and faithful servant! You have been faithful with a few things; I will put you in charge of many things. Come and share your master's happiness!'

Then the man who had received one bag of gold came. 'Master,' he said, 'I knew that you are a hard man, harvesting where you have not sown and gathering where you have not scattered seed. So I was afraid and went out and hid your gold in the ground. See, here is what belongs to you.' His master replied, 'You wicked, lazy servant! So you knew that I harvest where I have not sown and gather where I have not scattered seed? Well then, you should have put my money on deposit with bankers, so that when I returned I would have received it back with interest.

So take the bag of gold from him and give it to the one who has ten bags. For whoever has will be given more, and they will have an abundance. Whoever does not have, even what they have will be taken from them. And throw that worthless servant outside, into the darkness, where there will be weeping and gnashing of teeth."

Invest in Yourself

If you are not willing to invest in yourself, others won't be willing to invest in you either. Getting coaching was and still is one of the best decisions I have made for myself and my business. Coaching teaches me how to trust myself and helps keep me accountable. It's great to work on my own projects buts it's also really easy to not get to those projects, especially when you're first starting out. Even if it's not direct coaching, it could be online training.

Even though I'm talking about paid coaching here, I also believe there is value in investing in yourself in other ways, such as taking care of yourself (gym membership, massage, eating better), learning something new (buying a book, taking a course).

Be willing to put your money where your mouth is. If you say you want something different, you have to be willing to spend time and possibly money. Think about college for example. The expectation is that you invest with the anticipated outcome of getting a job that is better, than your options would be had you not attended college. There's no guarantee and even the coursework tends to not be enough. You then have to figure out a way to get hands on experience through an internship. We do all of this because it's what is expected.

What would happen if we sought education from someone that has done exactly what you want to do? To learn something that you know works, would you be interested in that? To be honest, that was a big barrier for me. I would seek resources high and low that were free, and then I heard my mentors say that they actually PAID for coaching. It knocked me down, but it also made so much sense. There is great wealth in attaining knowledge, but there is great wisdom is knowing how to attain that knowledge, and that's to go to the source. As we talked about aligning yourself with the right people, sometimes you have to pay to play and that's ok. Don't be afraid to use your dollars to support your dreams.

Let me tell you a little about how trusting God works. Remember when I told you about me fighting tooth and nail over going to Rosetta's Business Bootcamp? Well, that's actually where I met my coach. And what's even more, she's from Indianapolis, where I had just recently moved from and we share mutual friends. I was afraid to sow the initial seed of even going, but God answered my prayer through coaching. It doesn't stop there. I still needed to muster up the courage to actually invest in the coaching. My coach required me to be very honest with her about what I wanted from the relationship and how much I was willing to invest for those outcomes.

Honestly, I knew what I wanted to do before I even left Atlanta, but I was sinking further and further into my fear when I thought about telling her my number. It was scary because I wasn't completely sure about how it would fit in my budget and I didn't want to offend her with a low number. I was so worried about her feelings that I didn't realize the powerful step I was taking by 1) saying yes to myself and 2) being honest. Thinking back, the most important decision was the first one, saying "yes" to my investment. Saying "yes" meant that even if my coach had said no, I had already given myself permission to spend that money on coaching. It was out in the universe and I couldn't take it back!

Fortunately, she said she could work with me and actually appreciated my honesty. She was able to build a coaching experience tailored to my desired outcomes and price point. If I had held on to my seed, I would have continued to struggle alone. If I had held on to my seed, you wouldn't be reading this book. I had to decide to participate in the process. Do you want to be caught with your seed in your hand or in the ground?

BONUS: 3 "MUST HAVE" INVESTMENTS FOR YOUR BRAND

1) **Own your name** – Buy your domain name to save for your eventual website. Even if you don't have plans to run a business, you might have plans to find another job. A website can serve as an excellent online portfolio for the work that you have done and hope to do.
2) **Business cards** – Develop a simple business card for networking purposes. A lot of people take notes directly on business cards these days, with the quick tidbits you share during conversation, and you can start doing the same.
3) **Free cupcake** – If you do have plans to build a brand, you should think about developing a "free cupcake." A "free cupcake" is a resource that introduces your expertise that provides value to your intended audience in exchange for their email address.

These 3 investments are relatively inexpensive to create and can change over time as you learn more and grow your brand. Now you just have to leverage them to bring more opportunities that can support more investments.

God's Promise: "Be wise in the way you act towards outsiders; make the most of every opportunity." – Colossians 4:5

Leverage Your Network...and Launch

If you've made it to this point, can I just point out that I am proud that you are here. I hope that you are in the process of doing some of the "self" work or even completed some because it's vitally important in this phase. There are opportunities all around you and there are people that are just waiting for you to be ready to accept what they have waiting for you. You may even be experiencing some of those opportunities as you read these words or finally working on your project. And with this new found clarity, you may even start to feel like an imposter, a fraud, constantly worried that people will find out you're not good enough to represent your brand.

There's a name for that, called imposter syndrome. Imposter syndrome was first used by clinical psychologists Dr. Pauline Clance and Suzanne Imes, to refer to high-achieving individuals marked by the inability to internalize their accomplishments and a persistent fear of being exposed as a fraud. In other words, you feel inadequate, even when you know the opposite is true. We talked about this earlier, how the Enemy sneaks in and tries to convince you that even when your shit is popping, you think it just randomly happened or somebody else did it for you.

You may start to find yourself in circles where you don't quite feel like you belong or around people that you feel are so much better at handling life than you. First, it's not a bad thing because we need this to happen, in order for you to be around like-minded people that will inspire you and push you to be the highest version of yourself. Secondly, an elevated circle means a different network that you might not be exposed to if you're unwilling to be uncomfortable for a little while. Thirdly, you deserve to be there, even if you don't know why or still trying to figure out what you want to do, the fact that you are willing to take on new opportunities that stretch you, means you deserve to be there.

Society tells us that you have to put yourself out there and fight to the death to always be true to yourself, and that may turn into a need or desire to be perfect. But remember, God doesn't need you to be perfect. He needs you to be present and willing to accept the gifts and talents he gives you. Accept that you have the strengths and knowledge you need to move forward with whatever the vision is for your life, and that your success is worth you celebrating. Nothing just randomly happens to you. If you have ever had an opportunity to show your greatness, you will surely receive another and another, because you will seek them out. You won't be afraid to say yes to them, even when you are screaming 'no' on the inside.

You are not an imposter. You deserve to be doing the work that brings purpose to your life. Remember who you are and whose you are. Don't allow perfection to rob you of your journey. Identify with who you are now and be as authentic as you can in this season of your life, knowing that you change as you experience more. And don't hold back from who you are right now and the value that brings to the table. This is why I curse in this book. Because I curse in my real life. Do I curse like a sailor? Not all the time, not even half the time. Does that make me less of a God-fearing woman? No, it just means that I have to repent...a lot! But God's grace and mercy are sufficient.

It's important that you focus on the intrinsic value that you bring to this world. Only you can bring your perspective. Only you can leverage your story. You are in the right position. You do know the right people, even if you haven't met them yet. Stop comparing yourself to people that don't even know they are your competition. They don't deserve that much power over you. You're getting closer and closer to putting yourself out there and really walking by faith and not by sight. Are you ready to do the work?

God's Promise: "All hard work brings a profit, but mere talk leads only to poverty." – Proverbs 14:23

Do the Work – Don't think you have to do it all on your own

It's time to start really doing the hard work it takes to make this happen. Part of my message to you is that faith will take you to amazing places when you allow it to replace the doubt you feel about the next step to take when attacking your goals, the other side of that coin is focus. And with focus, comes intentional action. The Bible says this about lackluster effort:

> What good is it, my brothers and sisters, if someone claims to have faith but has no deeds? Can such faith save them? Suppose a brother or a sister is without clothes and daily food. If one of you says to them, "Go in peace; keep warm and well fed," but does nothing about their physical needs, what good is it? In the same way, faith by itself, if it is not accompanied by action, is dead. – James 2:14-17

Faith is not enough. Prayer is not enough. Fasting is not enough. Meditation is not enough. Although, all these things have a role, none of them take the place of a SMART action plan. Financial success is ultimately about money. Money is simply math. The math in business is Income – Expenses = Profit. None of which are dependent on faith, in the physical sense. So, while your spiritual journey is an important piece of the puzzle, you have to realize that it's just a piece, not the whole. The whole requires several components.

Let's switch gears to talk about somatic action. Somatic is really just a fancy word that means dealing with the body, distinguished from the mind or spirit. Here's another simple, yet true observation; this thing is going to take WORK. You may not know what the work is just yet, but you have to prepare yourself to be stretched and pulled spiritually, emotionally, mentally, and physically.

The good news about all of this is that you can handle it. You have been created to handle this. You now have the tools to boldly walk into your uncharted territory. You have always had the ability to choose what your tomorrows look like. But now, you understand the power of those choices. There's new opportunities to choose how you think about you, what you do, and who you want to be. Reading this book is your invitation. Doing the work is your RSVP. The question is: are you going to be a no-show to your own life?

On my commute one morning, I was listening to TD Jakes' podcast, *The Potters Touch*, and he was preaching about favor. He used the story of the blind man being healed as the context of his message. The story talks about how Jesus was traveling and came across a man that had been blind from birth. The disciples questioned who was responsible for his predicament, his own sins or the sins of his parents? Jesus basically told them to have several seats by replying, "Neither this man nor his parents sinned, but *this* (emphasis mind) happened so that the works of God might be displayed in him." He had to let them know that this "handicap" is nobody's fault, it's what the Father intended all along, so I can show you just how bad the Spirit is! And see, you are not the sum of your circumstances or the bad choices you made or even the bad choices your parents made. Everything in your life has been designed for you to cross paths with the one person or event that will change your life.

When it was time for the blind man to be healed, God made a paste from his spit and mud and told the man to put that on his eyes, go and wash in the water. I'm more of a "if I could just touch the hem of his garment" type but the man was <u>obedient</u> and was then able to see. I think this piece is important because the journey, the breakthrough, the healing doesn't always look like what we think it should look like, but we have to be obedient anyway. As I have learned through mentors and through my own spiritual growth, everything happens on a spectrum and it helps to be open and flexible with how success looks.

Back to the context of the story, once the blind man was healed, he went back to his neighborhood and the people started to wonder about him. Was it really him? How could he see now? He had to remind them that indeed, he was once blind, but now he could see. And it could only be explained because he crossed paths with the right person. People got curious and wanted to know how could this be, who is this person? You have to understand that at this time, Jesus, as the Messiah, was an unpopular belief. The law at the time wanted to know the truth about how this happened. The man had to keep proving his identity and that Jesus really healed him. They even kicked him out of his neighborhood, but God saw fit to find him. And he became a believer. The man lived his life, not knowing anything beyond his life as a blind man. He had grown up thinking that this was just the cards he was dealt. If he had not been blind, he wouldn't have had the opportunity to experience God's favor, to experience a new view, literally, of life. His favor came from his obedience. As will yours. Now that you see, you have a responsibility to forgive, heal and focus on the life that you know you deserve to live.

I know you feel that inkling in the back of your mind. That idea that just won't go away. The angst that won't allow you to sleep at night. Stop ignoring God's voice after you're done praying! You don't have to do this alone. I invite you to participate in a **complimentary accountability call** so we can connect personally. If you're reading a physical copy of this book (awesome), you can connect with me online at www.RebrandYourFear.com. I offer the call to be your sounding board, your unbiased filter to help you think through how you can change the narrative and implement simple solutions to these mundane life challenges that you're just tired of dealing with. We can work together to change your approach, create a plan of action and move forward with grace.

Again, I'll go back to the beginning, because until we know where we have come from, we won't know where we are going. This message is about love and purpose. There are people connected to your purpose that you don't even know yet. Even when it looks like you don't have anything to offer, you do. And everything you have now, can be used to stand on what seems like sinking sand and used to manifest what you don't have. God has given you permission to live a more abundant life, to conquer all the things that have held you back and live in the purpose that he has designed for you. God says that you are enough. Will you trust him?

You are ready for this and everything that you need is already inside of you. You have someone that loves you, trusts you, and needs you. That person is you. You have permission to let go of everything that has held you back up to this point. You have permission to use all those circumstances (good and bad) and stop just surviving and start thriving in your life. Whatever goals you have; you can accomplish them. Whatever fears you have, you can let them go. You don't have to constantly live in a state of confusion. The next step you take will be one of the most important steps you take. It will be the difference between sinking further into the life that is drowning you or standing firm on the promises of God. All you have to do is decide if you're worth it...and I know that you are. With love, Stephanie.

Action Plan Guide

- [ ] Create a 7-day SMART goal related to your bigger life goal. – **BONUS WORKSHEET!**
- [ ] Create a 30-day SMART goal related to your bigger life goal. – **BONUS WORKSHEET!**
- [ ] Write a "Signature" positive and personal affirmation.
- [ ] Create Pinterest vision board. Use **BONUS** WTF Journal as a guide to get clear on your boards.
- [ ] Write your new life narrative.
- [ ] Create a reward for accomplishing your 7-day and 30-day goal.
- [ ] Complete "Vet Your Ideas" Part 1 & 2 Worksheet. Decide on one direction.
- [ ] Review SWOT/PUSH analysis, identify 3 areas you need more knowledge/information.
- [ ] Create a self-care plan.
- [ ] Create a routine schedule that includes at least 10 hours per week on your life goals. – **BONUS TIME AUDIT!**
- [ ] Create a budget that includes tithing (include other means of giving).
- [ ] Develop the "Must Have" Brand Components
    - Business Card
    - Website
    - Free cupcake
- [ ] Email me your 7-day goal to receive a **complimentary** accountability session.

* TIME AUDIT WORKSHEET*

12:00 AM				
1:00 AM				
2:00 AM				
3:00 AM				
4:00 AM				
5:00 AM				
6:00 AM				
7:00 AM				
8:00 AM				
9:00 AM				
10:00 AM				
11:00 AM				
12:00 PM				
1:00 PM				
2:00 PM				
3:00 PM				
4:00 PM				
5:00 PM				
6:00 PM				
7:00 PM				
8:00 PM				
9:00 PM				
10:00 PM				
11:00 PM				

WTF JOURNAL PAGES

Where am I now?

faith

Where do I want to be?

How will I get there?

Where am I now?

family

Where do I want to be?

family

How will I get there?

Where am I now?

Where do I want to be?

How will I get there?

finances

Where am I now?

finances

Where do I want to be?

finances

How will I get there?

7-Day SMART GOAL WORKSHEET

Specific: _____

_____

_____

Measurable: _____

_____

_____

Attainable: _____

_____

_____

Realistic: _____

_____

_____

Time-bound: _____

_____

_____

(Within the next 7 days…ADD the date to make it real!)

30-Day SMART GOAL WORKSHEET

Specific: _____

_____

_____

Measurable: _____

_____

_____

Attainable: _____

_____

_____

Realistic: _____

_____

_____

Time-bound: _____

_____

_____

(Within the next 30 days…ADD the date to make it real!)

50 Things to Throw Away

1) Pens with no ink
2) Old food storage containers
3) Clothes that no longer fit
4) Take-out packets (ketchup, salt, etc.)
5) Mismatched socks
6) Old underwear/tired bras
7) Leftovers more than 5 days old
8) Old makeup
9) Shoes that don't fit or look good
10) Receipts you don't need
11) Old t-shirts
12) Gifts you don't like
13) Old towels
14) Expired medication
15) Dried-up nail polish
16) Bills you don't need to keep
17) Expired coupons
18) Old paperwork
19) DVDs you don't watch
20) Damaged clothes
21) Rusty/mismatched jewelry
22) Worn out sheets/bedding
23) Purse you never use
24) Old wallets you don't use
25) Manuals

26) Old craft supplies

27) Old/broken cell phones

28) Old spices

29) Email subscriptions you no longer find useful

30) Emails you don't need

31) Old textbooks you won't use

32) Old product boxes (i.e. Phones)

33) WIRE hangers

34) Toys

35) Old home décor

36) Things you bought and said you would return (Return, Sell, or Donate)

37) Knick Knacks (Grandma won't mind)

38) Old cords that don't go to anything

39) Old cleaning supplies

40) Beauty tools you don't use (i.e. curling irons, flat irons)

41) Shoe boxes

42) Old candles (use or throw away)

43) Keys that have no locks

44) Random batteries

45) Nearly empty bottles of stuff

46) Excess decks of cards (or loose ones)

47) Mementos from exes

48) Stockings with runs

49) Spare change (take it to the bank or put it in one place)

50) Unused picture frames

About the Author

Stephanie is a business owner, author, coach, speaker, and entrepreneur. She is often described as the PR specialist for the brand of YOU. Stephanie is a sought-after speaker, serving as the keynote presenter for several events (including the C.H. Russell Scholarship Banquet and Columbus/Bartholomew County NAACP's 2015 Graduate Reception). She has been honored with the Courage in Leadership Award and featured as an Emerging Leader in She Magazine.

Stephanie is a proud alumna of Indiana State. She earned a Bachelor's in Public Relations and Marketing, as well as Master's in Communication and Leadership Development. She currently serves as a program manager with the American Academy of Pediatrics working on childhood obesity initiatives. She is passionate about eliminating health disparities among underserved populations through the community and government programs.

When she's not writing, speaking, or supporting her entrepreneurial husband, Greg, she's often chasing the little man of her dreams, son Lynox, affectionately known as Nox, brushing up her vocabulary in sporadic games of Words with Friends, or spending way too much time on Pinterest dreaming of becoming a DIY'er.

References

Scriptures – All scriptures referenced are from the New International Version of the Bible.

Duhigg, C. (2014). *The Power of Habit: Why We Do What We Do in Life and Business*. New York: Random House.

Dyer, W. (1998). *Manifest Your Destiny: The Nine Spiritual Principles for Getting Everything You Want*. New York: Harper House.

www.ingramcontent.com/pod-product-compliance
Lightning Source LLC
LaVergne TN
LVHW051645080426
835511LV00016B/2501